Pelican Books
Pelican Geography and Environmental
Editor: Peter Hall

GW00711499

Resources for Britain's Future

Michael Chisholm is reader in economic geography at the
University of Bristol, a member of the Social Science
Research Council and Chairman of its subject committee
for human geography. Formerly he held appointments in
geography at the University of Ibadan, Nigeria, and
Bedford College, London, as well as in agricultural
economics at Oxford. He has been involved in consultancy
work in the field of regional development, both in the
United Kingdom and abroad. The focus of his research
and publication is location theory and regional
development, especially in the United Kingdom and with
special reference to transport. He has contributed papers
to numerous journals, including *Applied Statistics*, the *Farm
Economist*, *Geography*, the *Journal of the Town Planning
Institute*, *Oxford Economic Papers*, the *Transactions of
the Institute of British Geographers* and *Urban Studies*. His
published books are: *Rural Settlement and Land Use: an
Essay in Location* (1962), *Geography and Economics* (1966),
Regional Forecasting (as editor with A. E. Frey and
P. Haggett, 1971), *Spatial Policy Problems of the British
Economy* (as editor with G. Manners, 1971) and *Research
in Human Geography* (1971).

Resources for Britain's Future

A series from the *Geographical Magazine*

Edited for Penguin Books by
Michael Chisholm

Penguin Books Ltd, Harmondsworth,
Middlesex, England
Penguin Books Inc., 7110 Ambassador Road,
Baltimore, Maryland 21207, U.S.A.
Penguin Books Australia Ltd, Ringwood,
Victoria, Australia

First published in the *Geographical Magazine*
Copyright © the *Geographical Magazine*, 1969 and 1970
Published in Pelican Books 1972

Made and printed in Great Britain by
Butler & Tanner Ltd, Frome and London
Set in Monotype Times New Roman

This book is sold subject to the condition that
it shall not, by way of trade or otherwise, be lent,
re-sold, hired out, or otherwise circulated without
the publisher's prior consent in any form of
binding or cover other than that in which it is
published and without a similar condition
including this condition being imposed on the
subsequent purchaser

Contents

Contents

Preface

With the start of the 1970s, environmental pollution had become an issue of great public concern, both in this country and abroad. This is symbolized in the international Conservation Year and institutionalized in such ways as the annual report made by the President of the United States on the subject of pollution and related matters, and the standing Royal Commission established in the United Kingdom. Pollution and conservation provide good copy for the newspapers and material for dramatic television programmes. The Labour Party, in its June 1970 election campaign, promised tougher action to control pollution and preserve the environment: the Conservative government that was elected quickly amalgamated several government departments under the Secretary of State for the Environment. Yet the present collection of essays does not contain a single paper devoted specifically to this topic, a situation that may seem odd but is explicable. As originally conceived, the series of articles in the *Geographical Magazine* did not include one on pollution and conservation because a whole issue of the journal was to be devoted to this topic in the context of Conservation Year. Perhaps more important, pollution and conservation are only two facets of a much wider range of problems, namely, the evaluation, use and control of all resources for the benefit of the present and future generations.

The key issues may be stated quite briefly. First is the definition of acceptable standards. How high a level of local unemployment is tolerable, how nearly equal must educational opportunities be from one region to another, what degree of atmospheric pollution constitutes a hazard to health, how much space should there be for recreation? There is a general awareness that acceptable standards are not always available and that in other cases there is a serious threat to existing standards. More important, there is a widespread desire for an improvement – in communications, in the range of jobs available locally, in the cleanliness of beaches, etc. There is much less agreement, however, regarding the extent of improvement that should be sought and the rate at which it should be achieved. Second, however, is the manifest fact that higher standards will achieve little if the facilities are not available for use because the range of choice actually available to people is limited. As Peter Hall says, 'The job of the land use planner, then, is to multiply access to all sorts of opportunity within his planning region.' If this view is accepted, as surely it must be, then we as a nation are squarely on the horns of a dilemma.

Many of the decisions that concern the disposition of resources must rest with government, whether the question is how best to exploit the North Sea gas or on what scale the universities should be expanded, etc. Every one of us has an interest in the outcome of these decisions, either directly or indirectly, and on the face of it some form of centralized decision-making procedure will not only remain important but is likely to become increasingly necessary. On the other hand, one of the major justifications for our huge investment in the greatest single resource possessed by the nation – investment in the education of the population – is precisely the benefit received by the individual in being enabled to make choices. The exercise of choice implies both choosing between available possibilities and having a say in what the range of options should be. Furthermore, if choice is genuine, then unexpected fashions must be expected and provision made to cater for the pressures so generated.

Traditional Capitalism and traditional Socialism were both invented to cope with sets of problems different from those that now face us. In the context of resources for the future, it would be inappropriate to equate an increase in individual choice with Capitalism and an expansion in state control with Socialism. These two political dogmas are out-dated in many respects, not least in the naïve assumption that individuals play only one role in society when in fact we mostly play several, either sequentially in time or simultaneously. The Town and Country Planning machinery set up in 1947 and the framework for Regional Economic Planning established in 1964 and 1965, combined with the powers of central government, have not yet produced the right formula for government in the second half of the twentieth century. Perhaps, therefore, one of the great tasks for the 1970s is the search for better ways in which to allow greater individual freedom of choice in the use of resources while maintaining and enhancing the wider public interest.

The present collection of essays represents a contribution to this debate. The papers were all first published in the *Geographical Magazine* in 1969 and 1970, as a series under the title borne by this book and with myself acting in an advisory capacity. The papers have all been reprinted with the text substantially unchanged, except for minor alterations to bring the material up to date, to eliminate a few errors and to achieve consistency of presentation. Also, the order of the papers has been changed somewhat to exploit the fact that there are now no constraints imposed by deadlines for publication. As an underlying theme, the authors draw attention to the need for resource allocation decisions to be taken in a spatial frame and for an awareness of the spatial variation in the economic and social implications of these decisions. If these and related issues are squarely understood by all concerned, then one may hope that policy choices will be wiser than would otherwise be the case. It is with this hope that the authors, all of them geographers, have written.

MICHAEL CHISHOLM

The Geographical Task Ahead

by Michael Chisholm

Our present-day society is faced with a curious paradox: technology has enabled mankind to 'conquer' his physical environment far, far more effectively than ever before; yet never before has it been so necessary to study the nature and disposition of the natural resources that are available. This paradox has many roots, though the main one undoubtedly is the growth of technology and the increase in population, with the resulting increase in the power of mankind to spoil and destroy. There is, nevertheless, a wider and more general reason, since technological advancement implies both a greater pressure on the resources that are available and a wider choice in whether, where and when these pressures are to be allowed to operate. Because choices must be made, it is necessary to know what options are in fact available and also the criteria on which decisions are to be made. Thus the need to study our environment in all its aspects and to be aware of the relationships of one part to another.

However, the natural environment is only part of the wider setting in which we live and in practice much of the stimulus to take a new look at the mountains and moorlands, coalfields and climates, woodlands and waters, has been derived from a growing awareness of the social and economic problems associated with the seemingly inexorable spread of conurbations, the need to rebuild many of our 19th-century industrial cities and the problems arising from a changing occupational structure. Furthermore, we are being driven to the uncomfortable discovery that manipulation of the economy and of society is less easy than had been thought. In any case, the distinction between the natural and the social environment is artificial and if we are to organize ourselves for efficient production and happy living it is essential to consider the total environment.

It begins to appear that the 1960s will be regarded by future

11

historians as a decade that marked a number of important watersheds in the development both of attitudes and of institutions in this country, including two distinct but related sets of attitudes concerning the environment in which we live.

The first of these changes is related to the long evolution of the whole gamut of social legislation. The industrial revolution unleashed a host of powerful forces that created social inequalities of a magnitude that had not been experienced in this country before. Traditional forms of social security and means for the redistribution of incomes proved inadequate in the face of new demands being made upon them. For example, the Poor Law became necessary with the collapse of parish provision for the poor and destitute, and as a consequence of the growing mobility of the population. While the Poor Law replaced the parish almshouse, the Factory Acts and Truck Acts attempted to control the worst abuses of the new factory system. The disabilities attending illiteracy became increasingly evident and gradually during the later part of the last century and early in the present century schooling became universal and obligatory.

Increasing government expenditure outran the revenue sources that had served hitherto and new taxes were introduced, notably income tax. Direct taxation of incomes paved the way for systematic and effective redistribution of incomes from the wealthy to the poorer sectors but there was strong opposition to 'progressive' taxation and this feature of our society really only became established within living memory.

Electoral equality for women was achieved even more recently, nearly a hundred years after the Reform Act of 1832 that abolished the power exercised by those who could control the 'rotten boroughs'. During the 1920s and 1930s there was a slowing in the tempo of radical reform though consolidation of earlier achievements went on and the ground was prepared for another great step forward under the first Labour administration after the last war; perhaps the most important single post-war event was the establishment of the National Health Service.

All of these social changes have been conceived in the context of the 'two nations' that Disraeli described and Dickens decried; in the context of the class struggle that Marx postulated; in the context of the rights and dignity of man enshrined in the French Revolution. There can be no doubt that in this country enormous strides have been made in reducing the gap between social groups, though some commentators on the social scene, including Professor Titmuss (1962), consider that at least some progress has been less real than apparent.

It is a curious thing that as major wrongs are redressed, additional, but perhaps minor, wrongs come to light. As the inequalities between social classes have been narrowed, so has it become evident that the inequalities that remain are at least as much geographical as they are strictly 'class' in nature.

Perhaps the first major case of hardship and injustice that was recognized to be geographical was that of Ireland and parts of Scotland when the potato harvests failed in the 1840s. Unfortunately, the doctrines of Free Trade were paramount in Westminster and no effective relief was organized to ease the lot of thousands, including those who died of starvation or fled the country. In any case, the tragedy was regarded as something of a special case and both famine and pestilence were still thought of as afflictions to be endured. Even the successor problem of crofting in Scotland, examined by numerous commissions during this and the last century, has until recently been conceived as a single problem peculiar to one part of the country.

Public awareness of a *national* problem concerned with the allocation of resources between various parts of the country was not stimulated until the inter-war depression, which was attended by massive unemployment and demonstrations of discontent such as the Jarrow hunger march. Awareness of the problem approximately coincided in time with the realization that something could be done to solve it – Roosevelt's 'New Deal' in America had given convincing proof in practical terms, while Keynes had evolved economic concepts that pointed the way to action. It was only in 1934 that the first tentative steps were taken to organize a regional policy for employment, in the shape of the Special Areas – the predecessors of the present-day Development Areas. Special inducements have been available to encourage the expansion of employment in these Areas, but progress had not been great before the last war intervened. Regional policy in this sense has therefore been more of a post- than a pre-war phenomenon but it has been receiving steadily greater emphasis. Indeed, since the Local Employment Act of 1960, there has been a veritable deluge of legislation designed to foster development in the less fortunate regions and to curb it in the more prosperous ones.

In a wider context, Moser and Scott (1961) drew attention to the fact that there are distinct geographical differences in the quality of life and opportunity. Broadly speaking, they found that northern cities have a poorer housing stock, poorer educational facilities and achievements and a poorer health record than cities in southern Britain. Data published by the Commissioners for Inland Revenue show that the income before tax per taxpayer is two or three times greater in the London area than it is in Ulster; and unemployment in the Six Counties has consistently been 7 per cent or higher, compared with a national average of about 2 per cent.

The same point – that one's chance in life depends on where one is born – was made in a literary form by both Hoggart (1957) and Amis (1953) not very long after the war ended. The point has been reinforced by the race riots of Notting Hill, by the electoral upset at Smethwick when Patrick Gordon Walker lost to a more rabid opponent, and by similar events elsewhere. The country has become acutely aware of the dangers that attend the crystallization of society into geographically distinct groups. So much so, that the Government has recently embarked on a special programme to improve educational facilities in 'priority' areas, being specified localities in which the quantity and quality of schooling opportunities are far below acceptable standards.

Contemporaneously with developments that have exposed geographical inequalities in our society, a growing awareness of the condition dubbed by Galbraith as 'private affluence amidst public squalor' has developed. If we go back in history only a little over one hundred years, we shall see that the remarkable improvements in the standard of living and general welfare of the mass of ordinary folk about a century ago were associated not so much with rising personal income but with the organization of public services. New services took the form of clean water and water-borne sewage, the enforcement of minimum standards in the construction of dwellings, the spread of medical facilities and the setting up of an effective police force by Sir Robert Peel.

During the late 19th century and the early part of this century, much of the further gain in real income was taken in the form of increases in personal incomes, more so in the United States than elsewhere. Private affluence increases the range of choice available to an individual, choice as to what will be done, where and when. It also implies that an individual acquires much greater opportunity to do harm to his neighbours and also to his environment, whether deliberately or inadvertently, than he has had before.

These and related trends were recognized before the last war and permissive legislation had been enacted to give local authorities power to control changes in land use. But these powers lagged behind the vision of men like Ebenezer Howard, who earlier in the century had started the 'garden city' movement. It was not until the Town and Country Planning Act of 1947 that a reasonably comprehensive view was taken of the national need to organize resources in a proper spatial manner. Even then, the full magnitude of the problems confronting us had not become evident. Colin Buchanan (1963) alerted the country to the intra-urban problems of coping with the motorcar. Manchester's attempts to draw even more water from the Lake District to ease an apparently insatiable thirst were thwarted only in the House of Lords. This episode brought into the open the need to regard water supplies as a national resource and not merely as a series of local headaches, a need that had hitherto been evident to only a small band of discerning men. The more recent Stansted fiasco forced the Government to recognize that the whole machinery of decision-making was based on false premises and provision has now been made for major investment decisions to be reviewed in a much wider context.

Meanwhile, the steady spread of a fortnight's annual paid holiday to all sections of the working population, the prospect that three weeks will be general practice before long, the shortening of the working week from five and a half or six days to five, and the increasing ownership of cars, has unleashed a horde of holiday-makers into the countryside. The concept of green belts around the major cities is now seen to be inadequate and thoughts are turning to the

1 *and* 2. *Regional contrasts are already stark but are rapidly becoming stronger, particularly in the important sphere of housing. A million new homes are built every three years, but old industrial northern towns like Burnley are likely to retain their 19th-century housing areas for many years to come. The landscaped layout of a housing estate in Kent shows what can be done. But should it be merely the luck of the draw as to who shall live in areas of growth and can therefore enjoy the best of modern amenities?*

integrated development of a variety of recreational facilities. A major example which is now just getting under way is the conversion of the Lea Valley near London into an open-air leisure area to cater for a million visitors a year. Even this imaginative scheme must be seen in terms of other opportunities for city-dwellers to enjoy the fresh air such as the new marina at Brighton, skiing at the thriving Aviemore centre and the observation of nature on the Brecon Beacons. One potentially important facet of life that the Countryside Commission is having investigated is the growing custom of owning two homes, a habit that clearly affects the countryside but also the pattern of urban development and the scale of traffic movement.

In a nutshell, our society is moving into an era in which the health and happiness of our people will increasingly depend on the success we have in preventing 'public squalor' and replacing it with convenience, range of choice and beauty. In this endeavour, it is essential to consider the country as a whole, so that the various parts may most effectively be used for the benefit of the whole society. This means getting beyond the clichés to make hard decisions. This is no easy matter as may be illustrated by the referendum held among the inhabitants of Barnstaple in Devon when London wanted to transfer some of its overspill population to that worthy town. The referendum did not extend to those who were potential immigrants; had it done so, the decision to reject the scheme might have been reversed. But how does one identify all the interested parties?

In the spirit of this essay, the American Institute of Planners marked the first fifty years of its existence by mounting a two-year study (1967–69) of the next fifty years, to try to identify the major social and environmental issues and their possible solution. In Britain we have had a Central Unit for Environmental Planning and, in its place since 1970, a Secretary of State for the Environment.

It seems quite clear that there will be a continuing and growing interest in the nature and disposition of the nation's resources, so that better use may be made of what we have (Chisholm and Manners, 1971). In terms of national planning, it is now accepted that the fullest possible use of labour supplies is essential. To this end, regional planning lays much emphasis on the reduction of unemployment in Ulster, Scotland, Wales and elsewhere. Of equal importance is to raise the proportion of the population that offers its services on the labour market so that activity rates in the less prosperous regions can be lifted nearer the national average. A publication by the Ministry of Transport (1969) promises that the transport needs of the country are at last being seen in national terms. However, despite these encouraging signs and the existence of the machinery that is embodied in the Regional Economic Planning Councils and Boards and in the Town and Country Planning Acts, there is still a long way to go before the full geographical implications of and potential for development are realized.

References

Amis, K., *Lucky Jim*, Gollancz, 1953, Penguin Books, 1961.

Buchanan, C. D., *Traffic in Towns*, Ministry of Transport, 1963, Penguin Books, 1964.

Chisholm, M., and Manners, G. (eds), *Spatial Policy Problems of the British Economy*, CUP, 1971.

Galbraith, J. K., *The Affluent Society*, Hamish Hamilton, 1958, Penguin Books, 1962.

Hoggart, R., *The Uses of Literacy*, Chatto & Windus, 1957, Penguin Books, 1958.

Howard, E., *Garden Cities of Tomorrow*, Faber & Faber, 1902.

Keynes, J. M., *The General Theory of Employment, Interest and Money*, Macmillan, 1936.

Ministry of Transport, *Roads for the Future – a New Inter-Urban Network*, HMSO, 1969.

Moser, C. A., and Scott, W., *British Towns: A Statistical Study of Their Social and Economic Differences*, Oliver & Boyd, 1961.

Titmuss, R. M., *Income Distribution and Social Change: a Study in Criticism*, Allen & Unwin, 1962.

The Framework of Change

Population: Basic Trends and Problems

by Richard Lawton

In a country of 55,000,000 people living on only 22,700,000 hectares, where competition for land is acute, people are arguably Britain's greatest single asset, now and in the future. In the 1930s a falling birth rate, accentuated by the depression, and an age and sex imbalance, resulting from the toll of the battlefields of World War I, reduced the natural rate of increase of population. While numbers grew because of a falling death rate and increased expectation of life, the future prospects for growth were poor. A predicted decline of Britain's population in the future led to the setting up in 1944 of a Royal Commission on Population which reported in 1949. Its most optimistic forecast for England's population at the end of the century was 40,000,000, its least only 28,000,000, and it supported social measures to increase family size and safeguard child health.

In the event these gloomy forecasts were confounded. The upsurge of births in the immediate post-war years did not prove to be a short-lived 'bulge' but part of a trend to a higher, though fluctuating, birth rate. After a fall in the early 1950s, the birth rate climbed to a level far above that of the inter-war years. During the early 1960s it almost reached the proportions of the post-war 'baby boom', though birth rates have again fallen since 1964, perhaps due to the contraceptive pill. However, they are still considerably higher than between the wars (see Table p. 24). Earlier and more universal marriage and changed social attitudes have all contributed to higher fertility and somewhat larger average families. In England and Wales the average age of first marriage for women, 25·5 years in 1926–30, fell to 23·3 in 1956–60 and is now 22·5: the equivalent Scottish figures are 25·9, 23·6 and 22·5. The proportion of women aged 15–49 who had experience of matrimony increased in England and Wales from 529 per 1,000 in 1931 to 700 in 1961 and was 697 in 1967; in Scotland the proportion rose from 483 to 677 and at present is 686 (rates per 1,000 women 16–49).

Trends in birth rates and death rates in Britain, 1931–70

	Average births per 1,000			
	1931–35	1946–50	1956–60	1966–70
England and Wales	15·0	18·0	16·4	16·9
Scotland	18·2	20·0	19·2	18·0
	Average deaths per 1,000			
	1931–35	1946–50	1956–60	1966–70
England and Wales	12·0	11·8	11·6	11·7
Scotland	13·2	12·6	12·0	12·1

Meanwhile people are living longer. The expectation of life, in 1930–2 only 58·7 years for men and 62·9 for women in England and Wales, and 56·0 and 59·5 in Scotland, is now 69·1 and 75·2 for England and Wales and 67·4 and 73·6 for Scotland. The implications of this three-fold increase – of married couples and of senior and junior citizens – are enormous and are reflected in the high post-war population increase and the much faster rate of growth of households. The number of households in England and Wales increased by 28·2 per cent between 1931 and 1951 as against a population increase of 9·5 per cent; corresponding increases of 12·0 and 5·3 per cent respectively occurred between 1951 and 1961, and of 4·9 and 2·2 per cent between 1961 and 1966. Heavy pressures have been placed upon housing, hospitals, schools and other social services, the true implications and cost of which are only now being recognized fully.

For over one hundred years from the early 19th century Britain was a net 'exporter' of people. Though many immigrants came to

Britain from Ireland, central and eastern Europe and elsewhere overseas, creating culturally varied colonies in many cities, this was more than offset by massive emigration leading to a net migration loss of nearly 3,000,000 people between 1841 and 1911. This mainly outward flow was reversed in the 1930s as emigration to the Dominions slowed down and there was an influx of refugees – many of them Jewish – from Europe, a trend accentuated by war.

In the last decade there has been a new wave of immigration of British Commonwealth citizens from the Caribbean, India and Pakistan, and, to a lesser extent, tropical Africa. This trend added nearly half a million people between 1958 and 1962, when it was slowed down by the Commonwealth Immigrants Act. In fact, in the period 1965–9, net immigration from the New Commonwealth amounted to 296,000, but this was insufficient to offset other emigration and there was a net loss overall of 204,000 in the period.

The precise results of this immigration are hard to assess in the absence of adequate immigration and census statistics. To elicit further information questions were asked in the 1971 Census about the year of entry into Britain of those not born in the UK and the country of birth of both parents of all the enumerated population. Immigration has, however, brought new workers to many types of job – particularly in hospitals, railways and textile mills – and new societies to the inner areas of many of our cities. With a generally youthful age-structure in an active phase of family formation, with different social customs and, sometimes, language, these new Britons are often regarded with suspicion and, regrettably, at times with dislike.

Like all immigrant communities they tend to be closely concentrated in particular districts; areas with high proportions of coloured immigrants include West Yorkshire (especially Bradford, Huddersfield and Dewsbury), the West Midlands (with large concentrations in Wolverhampton, Birmingham, Leamington, Warley and Walsall), parts of the East Midlands (notably Bedford, Derby and Leicester) and particularly the central boroughs of Greater London (where Brent, Lambeth, Hackney, Haringey, Islington and Hammersmith all have an estimated coloured population of more than 1 in 20), though other towns of South-east England (such as Slough,

25

High Wycombe and Hitchin) also have considerable proportions of immigrants.

The present coloured population of Britain is estimated at 1·3 million (1970): the impact on future population, especially in those areas where immigrants are at present concentrated, has been a cause of concern and controversy. The first official figures of immigrant births show that 11·8 per cent of all births in England and Wales between April and September 1969 were to foreign-born mothers, 3·2 per cent of whom were Irish, and an estimated 2·8 per cent other white, leaving a maximum 5·8 per cent of births to coloured immigrant mothers. It is true that in some areas of high immigrant concentrations much higher proportions were recorded; for example in some London Boroughs nearly 30 per cent of births in this period were to mothers from new Commonwealth countries.

Undoubtedly their present rate of increase is high: but there is no evidence to suggest that this growth is higher than among others of similar age-structure and social background, or that their future rates of increase will differ significantly from more general predictions. It is unlikely that they and their descendants will exceed 3 to 3·5 million by the end of the century, though figures of 4·5 to 7 million have been quoted albeit with little supporting evidence. By then mobility and inter-marriage will probably have absorbed many newcomers into our already varied society and spread them more evenly throughout our cities.

Collectively, these trends have led to a very different population situation from that envisaged in the 1940s. Despite a recent fall in birth rate and a reversal of the inward balance of migration, the expectation is that by A.D. 2000 the population of Britain will be some 64,000,000 – as against a 1964 estimate of 73,000,000. Of these, according to the 1969 mid-year estimate, 59,000,000 will be in England and Wales. Not surprisingly, doubts have been cast on our ability to feed, house and provide space for recreation for such numbers. Yet, in a country which depends for its livelihood on skilled manpower, a growing population is also an asset. Undoubtedly the situation presents a great challenge in planning the use of resources of land and manpower, and requires the urgent consideration and implementation of an effective population policy for Britain.

Within this general framework there are considerable contrasts in natural change and mobility of population. Some of these are generic in character, as between town and country or city centre and suburb; others mirror the varying economic fortunes of regions of widely varying character.

In rural areas, especially those remote from urban amenities and poor in agricultural resources, over a century of depopulation and the migration of young people has progressively sapped vitality and led to an ageing population in which deaths exceed births. This is the case in many parts of the Scottish Highlands, Wales, the northern Pennines and south-west England. But prosperous agricultural areas of eastern England – including east Yorkshire, Lincolnshire, the Fenland and Norfolk – have also experienced persistent losses (Figure 1). In such areas jobs are few and, as farms are amalgamated into larger units, are becoming fewer, especially in the upland areas. Services run down; settlements become less viable and may even die out altogether. The future is bleak, though forestry and recreational use may inject new vigour into a few of these communities.

Those rural areas within reach of the towns retain population by commuting: even a small town like Aberystwyth may draw labour from a wide rural area. The big cities influence considerable rural hinterlands which, though creating problems in land-use planning, help to retain population and bring wages into the villages. Overspill from the towns has brought what Sir Dudley Stamp described as 'adventitious population' into this rural-urban fringe, leading to post-war increases in population. Such trends will continue and they emphasize the need for the integration of planning and services with adjacent towns. This dependence on town jobs may be seen in the high proportion of daily movement of people from rural districts throughout an axial belt from Greater London to south Lancashire-west Yorkshire, and around the very highly urbanized areas of South Wales, north-east England and central Scotland (Figure 2).

After 150 years of rapid growth, the cities of Britain are bursting at the seams and need retailoring to the shape of the late 20th century. Thirty-five per cent of Britain's population live in the seven official conurbations, 60 per cent are concentrated in the axial belt and a further 8,000,000 – about 15 per cent – in central Scotland, north-east England and South Wales. These areas are growing in population and employment and will certainly continue to do so in the future, with a corresponding attraction of jobs in both manufacturing and service industries. However, as cities expand so do the problems of living and working in them. Zoning and redevelopment of land for industry, commerce and housing, journeys to work and access to recreational facilities, and new standards of living, are all changing our concept of city life. They demand new approaches to its design and organization.

Clearing of inner-city slums and rehousing has led to outward movement from all our major cities (Figure 1). While the worst excesses of inter-war suburban sprawl have been avoided, post-war suburbs have led to much short-range migration and high rates of population growth around all large towns. Despite new peripheral industrial estates, it has not been easy to match jobs to people, especially since most households now have more than one wage-earner. Consequently, journeys to work in and around cities have grown more complex and more time-consuming.

Tighter control of housing development in towns has restricted continuous outward growth, especially around London, by the designation of 'green belts'. Beyond these open areas has grown an outer suburbia of dormitory settlements characterized by rapid increases of population and some of the highest rates of mobility. With their preponderance of young households, rates of natural increase are high on both local authority and private housing estates. In an attempt to prevent unlimited suburban sprawl, especially around Greater London, new towns have been established in which not only homes but jobs are available. Despite their success – a tribute to our planners – provision of jobs in the London new towns has lagged behind provision of homes, and there is still a good deal

Figure 1　Total population change in Britain, 1951–61. The regional trends of the 1960s have closely followed those shown in this map. In the 1950s, decreases of population were experienced throughout rural Britain, especially in Highland Britain. The central areas of cities and conurbations lost population to the suburbs. Regional growth was most marked in the Midlands and South-east, and in many old industrial areas population declined absolutely or relatively (through migration losses).

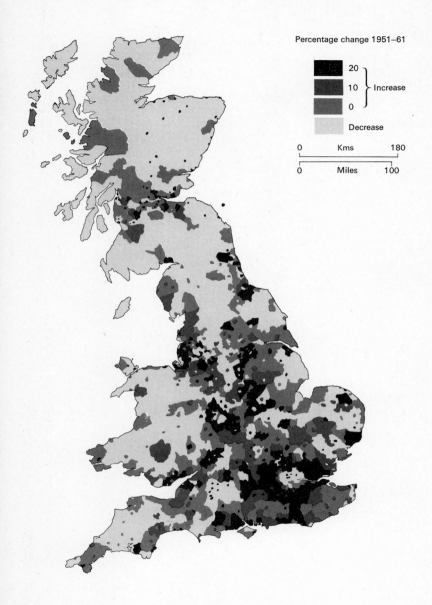

Percentage change 1951–61

20 ⎫
10 ⎬ Increase
0 ⎭

Decrease

0　　　Kms　　　180
0　　　Miles　　　100

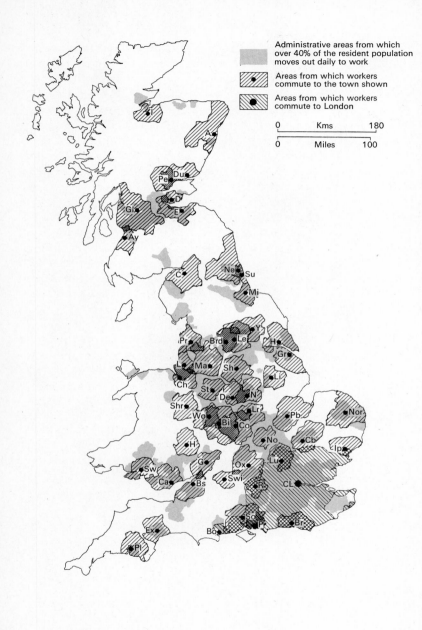

Administrative areas from which
over 40% of the resident population
moves out daily to work

Areas from which workers
commute to the town shown

Areas from which workers
commute to London

0   Kms   180
0   Miles   100

of commuting from them into London. Similar problems exist in the provincial conurbations where proportionately less has been achieved. In north-west England, for example, despite acute shortages of land for housing overspill from Merseyside and Greater Manchester, new town development has been slow. Liverpool's new towns at Skelmersdale and Runcorn are too near the city to have independent existence; Manchester still awaits its new towns. For both populations the Preston-Leyland-Chorley new town (Ribbleton) offers hope of homes and jobs for thousands of slum dwellers. Undoubtedly the scale of provision of present new towns throughout Britain has been too conservative and much bigger communities are now being planned, especially in the South-east.

Many of the problems of population growth and movement are common to all urban and industrial regions. But throughout the 20th century there have been other distinctive regional trends in population which are likely to persist over the next generation. The dominant feature, commented upon by the Barlow Report in 1940, is still the drift of population to the South-east.

The depression of the 1930s hastened the decline of the coalfields and coal-based industrial areas on which much of the population growth of Victorian Britain was centred. In 1932, at the depth of the depression, unemployment rates were well above the national average of 22 per cent in Wales, Scotland and northern England; indeed, in such towns as Jarrow or Merthyr Tydfil they rose to over 70 per cent. Massive out-migration followed as people moved to the more prosperous areas of the Midlands, London and the South-east, where unemployment rates were often only half the national average. The focusing of industrial and commercial growth in these fortunate regions attracted population; this in turn attracted consumer and service industries. The gap between the two Britains widened.

Figure 2   Some features of the journey to work in Britain, 1961. The local authority areas which supplied over 100 workers daily to the towns indicated are shaded. Central London – which drew in 1,250,000 workers daily – had by far the biggest hinterland. The background shading, showing local authority areas from which over 40 per cent of resident workers travelled daily, indicates the dependence on a few areas of job concentration.

These problems are clearly reflected in migration of population between the major regions. Between 1921 and 1951, the South-east, as now broadly defined for planning purposes, had a net gain by migration of nearly 1,200,000 people. The Midlands, after a net loss in the 1920s, gained over 300,000 between 1931 and 1951, while the South-west gained slightly less. In contrast, all other major regions lost population by migration: 912,000 from the north of England; 434,000 from Wales; and 675,000 from Scotland. Within the whole of north-western Britain the only areas of gain were around the large cities.

One of the principal concerns of post-war planning has been to diminish the wide gap in job opportunities between the regions. Control of new manufacturing industry through the Board of Trade's Industrial Development Certificates, and direct incentives for industry moving to Development Areas have perhaps slowed down but not arrested the south-east drift. Indeed, between 1951 and 1961, the South-east gained over 500,000, an increase of 3·1 per cent, by migration, though Greater London lost some of its population by movement from the overcrowded inner areas of the conurbation (Figure 1). The South-west with a gain of 78,000 and the Midlands with 126,000 continued to share in this growth.

Prediction of future growth and especially of future migration is difficult, but all evidence points to a continuation of these trends. Unemployment rates have been consistently below the national average in the Midlands and South-east since the war, and most parts of these regions have had a general labour shortage. Estimates by the South-east Development Council suggest that between 1967 and 1981 the region will increase its population by 2,000,000. A further 4,000,000 may be added by A.D. 2000 to reach a population in the South-east of 23,000,000 – over one-third of the estimated total for Britain.

Such massive increases should be compared with the total target population of 638,000 for London's present new towns. Clearly, several new cities are required, and, in fact, are presently being planned, which will each accommodate up to half a million people, and be large enough and far enough from London to avoid its domination. Yet there can be little doubt that the powerful pull of London will continue to generate commuting to the centre, while much of the most rapid growth of population will occur on the periphery of the region.

Even though large numbers of new jobs have been created in Development Areas, especially in central Scotland, north-east England, Merseyside and South Wales, post-war unemployment in these areas has persistently remained above the national rates. A relatively high rate of natural increase, particularly in Scotland and northern England, has added to the problem so that migration losses have continued. Between 1951 and 1961 Scotland had a net loss of over 300,000 people. Only in Wales had the outward flow been staunched to a modest 49,000. Projections of future trends suggest that out-migration from Wales may decline still further and that from Scotland fall to less than half its present level by 1981. The outlook for northern England remains poor, with an estimated migration loss of 280,000 between 1968 and 1981.

This does not imply that total regional populations will decline or that every part of these regions will be affected equally. In north-west England, for example, although the estimated loss by migration may be 100,000 between 1968 and 1981, the region's total population is likely to increase through high birth rates from 6,755,000 to 7,115,000. This increase will occur mainly in the zone between Merseyside and Greater Manchester and will lead to increased concentration in an already congested area.

National and regional trends of population overlie detailed changes of great complexity. Agriculture now employs less than 4 per cent of workers and, though 20 per cent live in administrative Rural Districts, perhaps as little as 10 per cent of the total population of Britain is truly rural. Expanding cities both supply population for ever-wider suburban hinterlands and draw from them many workers: these tendencies are reflected both in complex patterns of commuting and high levels of residential mobility, much of which is on a local scale. In Merseyside, for example, an average 1 in 15 of the 1966 census population – commonly more than 1 in 10 – changed residence in the previous year. Such mobility is likely to persist and makes an estimate of future population distribution difficult.

The dramatic demographic changes since the war and their effects

33

on the predictions of the Royal Commission on Population stress the need for constant revision of population forecasts in the light of the latest figures of births, deaths and migration and highlight the urgency of developing a population policy. Such a policy is of great importance for economic, social and planning purposes. Thus after a generation in which both young and old dependents have increased, we can look forward to a period up to 1981 when there will be a further 1,000,000 people in the workforce. Over half this workforce, it is expected, will be female. Providing employment, housing and services most appropriately for these people will be one of the more powerful factors influencing the geography of Britain in the 1970s.

References

OFFICIAL SOURCES
1. General Register Office, London (for England and Wales) and Edinburgh (for Scotland): regular estimates are issued by the Registrars General of which the most important are the *Quarterly Returns*, the *Annual Estimate of the Population*, the *Annual Statistical Review* (with tables, commentary and supplements covering a wide range of population and medical topics), and the *Decennial Supplement* to the *Census* (on types of mortality).
2. A full census for England and Wales and for Scotland was taken in 1961 (with separate county and many subject volumes published 1961–9); a more limited sample census was taken in 1966 for 10 per cent of households. The most recent full census was taken on 25 April 1971.
3. The following Royal Commission Reports are of great value in the study of population evolution: *Royal Commission on the Distribution of the Industrial Population, 1937–39* (Barlow Report) (1940, reprinted 1963); *Royal Commission on Population, 1944–49* (1949).
4. A valuable new source of general population, social and economic statistics for the United Kingdom is *Social Trends* No. 1, 1970 (HMSO, 1970, for the Central Statistical Office). Edited by Muriel Nissel this is to be revised and published annually.

GENERAL REFERENCES. This includes only a brief outline of books on major British population topics. There are, in addition, a great many specialist papers, some of which are referred to in the books listed.
Benjamin, B., *The Population Census*, Heinemann, 1969.
　　　Demographic Analysis, Allen & Unwin, 1968.
Carrier, N. H., and Jeffrey, J. R., *External Migration: a study of the available statistics, 1815–1950*, General Register Office; Studies on Medical and Population Subjects No. 6, HMSO, 1953.

Population: Basic Trends and Problems

Davison, R. B., *Commonwealth Immigrants*, OUP, 1964.

Freeman, T. W., *The Conurbations of Great Britain* (Second edition), Manchester University Press, 1966.

Glass, R., *Newcomers: the West Indians in London*, Allen & Unwin, 1960.

Howe, G. M., *National Atlas of Disease Mortality in the United Kingdom* (Revised and enlarged edition), Nelson, 1970.

Isaac, J., *British Post-war Migration*, CUP, 1954.

Marsh, D. C., *The Changing Social Structure of England and Wales, 1871–1961* (Revised edition), Routledge & Kegan Paul, 1965.

Newton, M. P., and Jeffrey, J. R., *Internal Migration: Some aspects of population movement within England and Wales*, General Register Office: Studies on Medical and Population Subjects, No. 5, HMSO, 1951.

Osborne, R. H., 'Population', pp. 331–57 of Watson, J. W., and Sissons, J. B. (eds.), *The British Isles: a systematic geography*, Nelson, 1964.

Roberts, B. C., and Smith J. H. (eds.), *Manpower Policy and Employment Trends*, Bell, 1966.

Rose, E. J. B. *et al.*, *Colour and Citizenship: a report on British Race Relations*, OUP, 1969.

Rowntree, J. A., *Internal Migration*, General Register Office: Studies on Medical and Population Subjects No. 11, HMSO, 1957.

Saville, J. *Rural Depopulation in England and Wales, 1851–1951*, Routledge & Kegan Paul, 1957.

POPULATION POLICY. The growing problems of population pressure have given rise to much recent discussion and a Parliamentary Select Committee, set up in January 1969 to study this question, reported in May 1971. Aspects of population pressure and suggestions for a population policy for Britain are discussed in:

Taylor, L. R. (ed.), *The Optimum Population for Britain*, Institute of Biology Symposium No. 19, Academic Press, 1970.

Glass, D. V., *et al*, *Towards a Population Policy for the United Kingdom* (Supplement to *Population Studies*), The Population Investigation Committee, London School of Economics, 1970.

First Report from the Select Committee on Science and Technology, Session 1970-71. *Population of the United Kingdom*, HMSO, 1971.

Farming for an Urban Nation

by Terry Coppock

The United Kingdom occupies a unique position among the developed countries, with only 3 per cent of the working population engaged in agriculture, with less than half a hectare of agricultural land per head and with imports providing half the nation's food supply. These circumstances, a consequence of early industrialization, limited land resources and a policy of cheap food for the urban population, underlie both the present and the future shape of British agriculture and have a special relevance as Britain's third application to join the European Economic Community is considered in Brussels.* Decisions as to the 'right' proportion of home-produced food and the 'right' share of national resources that should be devoted to agriculture are essentially political, but they should be based on an appreciation of the variety of problems which agricultural changes pose in different parts of the country.

Predicting the future shape of British agriculture must be a highly speculative undertaking. The rate of technical progress in both agriculture and the food manufacturing industries, the changing patterns of domestic consumption as living standards rise, the hazards of estimating population trends, and uncertainty about future government policy, all influence development. Ploughless agriculture and synthetic foodstuffs are but two of the technical possibilities which may have major consequences for British farming. Decisions taken by the European Economic Community, both on the United Kingdom's application and on agricultural policies and price levels within the Community, will also affect British agriculture, although, in the short term, they are more likely to accelerate or retard trends already apparent than to initiate new developments.

An estimate of the future place of farming must begin with an assessment of the achievements of the past thirty years. It is increas-

* See p. 166.

ingly difficult to recall the state of British agriculture in the 1930s. A prolonged, almost continuous period of depression had culminated in a world economic crisis and the first tentative attempts by a British government in peace time to influence the course of agricultural production. Lack of resources for both farmers and landowners had led to widespread neglect of land and buildings, the area under crops had fallen to the lowest level ever recorded, and more than two-thirds of all food supplies were imported. This situation was transformed by the need to increase home food production during World War II, by the acceptance by governments of an obligation to maintain 'a stable and efficient agricultural industry', and by what has been called 'the current agricultural revolution'. From a national farm reduced by nearly 800,000 hectares, British farmers now produce half the food required to support, at an appreciably higher standard of living, a population which has increased by 7,000,000. The United Kingdom is today virtually self-sufficient in eggs, milk, potatoes, pork and poultry meat, and, with the exception of butter, the proportion of nearly every other food that is home-produced has risen sharply.

It is impossible to determine how much of this gain in agricultural production can be attributed to technical advances in agriculture and how much to government support since some subsidies have been designed to promote land improvement or desirable practices, and their share of the subsidy bill of some £250,000,000 a year has been increasing. The provision of price guarantees for all major products of British farming has also contributed to increased production. These deficiency payments represented a quarter of net farm income in 1968–9. The annual review of the level of government support is thus of major importance to farmers and, whilst there is debate about the form of support, a reversion to a policy of *laissez-faire* cannot be contemplated. The form of future government aid will be a major determinant of the geography of British agriculture in the 1970s and 1980s.

New, higher-yielding varieties of crops, better control of weeds and pests, improved livestock, better feed conversion rates, and greater stocking densities through better grass management have contributed to the marked upward trend in yields of crops, livestock and livestock products. Agricultural net output increased by 60 per

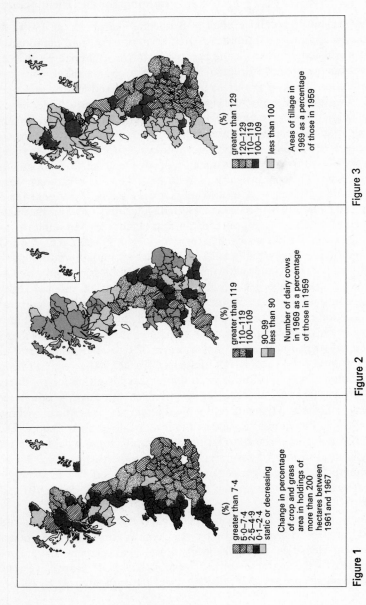

(%)
▨ greater than 7·4
▨ 5·0–7·4
▨ 2·5–4·9
▨ 0·1–2·4
▨ static or decreasing

Change in percentage
of crop and grass
area in holdings of
more than 200
hectares between
1961 and 1967

Figure 1

(%)
▨ greater than 119
▨ 110–119
▨ 100–109
▨ 90–99
▨ less than 90

Number of dairy cows
in 1969 as a percentage
of those in 1959

Figure 2

(%)
▨ greater than 129
▨ 120–129
▨ 110–119
▨ 100–109
▨ less than 100

Areas of tillage in
1969 as a percentage
of those in 1959

Figure 3

cent between the 1930s and the mid-1950s and has since risen by a further 40 per cent. Part of this gain can be attributed to the improvements in agricultural land through drainage and reclamation and to greatly increased use of lime and fertilizer, which rose six-fold and eight-fold respectively between 1939 and 1965.

Increased output has contributed to the steady improvement in labour productivity, but the greater part of this increase is due to the replacement of men by machines; since the late 1940s the number of agricultural workers has fallen by more than half, while the number of tractors has more than doubled. Under the stimulus of smaller profit margins in the past decade, productivity in agriculture has increased twice as fast as in manufacturing industry and mechanization has continued in the 1960s. Old machines are constantly replaced by more powerful models and although there are now fewer tractors, specialized equipment, such as grain driers and sugar beet harvesters, is being more widely adopted. In livestock farming large investment in new buildings has helped to improve output per man. The tendency of livestock farming to go under cover and for some processing to take place on the farm has contributed to the increasing factory-like appearance of many farmsteads. These trends can be expected to continue but with a smaller labour force increasingly concentrated on the larger farms in eastern and southern Britain.

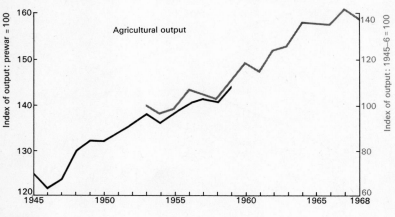

Figure 4

Undoubtedly much more could be produced, as the wide variation in yield between farms situated on similar land shows; but not all imports of temperate products can be replaced, for some differ in quality, such as the imported hard wheats required for bread-making. Additional incentives and resources would be necessary for any rapid increase in production; a National Economic Development Office committee has estimated that, given an investment of £230 million, agricultural output could rise by one-fifth between 1967–8 and 1972–3. Whether such an increase is desirable is another question, and it has been government policy since the mid-1950s that agricultural expansion should be selective, with greater regard for costs of production and market requirements than in the period of food shortage during and after the war. With some commodities, notably milk, there are already problems of over-supply and the government has limited the quantities to which price guarantees apply; farmers have had to absorb a substantial proportion of rising costs by greater efficiency.

There is evidence that rising yields and productivity are widening the difference between the better and poorer land. Greater specialization and the increasing size of farms and enterprises are also tending

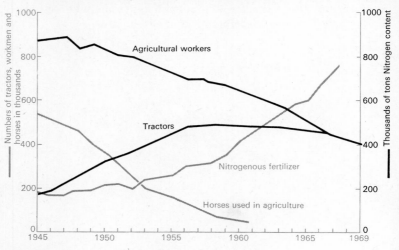

Figure 5

to sharpen regional contrasts. Mechanization has provided the opportunity, and pressure on profit margins the incentive, to increase the scale of individual enterprises. There are fewer producers of nearly every product and the average size of enterprise is rising; since 1954 the number of holdings with dairy cows has fallen by nearly two-thirds and the average herd doubled in size, while the number of pig keepers has more than halved and the size of herd trebled. As farmers abandon less profitable enterprises the others are becoming more specialized. Egg production is a good example, where the large specialist holding is replacing the barnyard flock and one producer expects to account for a quarter of all output within five years. With broilers, too, more than half the national flock is in units of 50,000 birds or more. Intensive methods and the large scale of

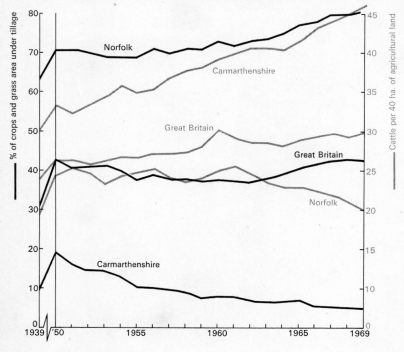

Figure 6

41

3. *Since the introduction of the combine harvester, large fields and vestigial hedgerows are becoming increasingly characteristic of Britain's arable areas. This field on Salisbury Plain is swiftly harvested by five combines.*

production have led to much discussion about factory farming and it becomes increasingly difficult to draw a line between agriculture and industry; but true factory farming still concerns only a small minority of farms.

Farms are getting larger and farmers fewer, and these changes also accentuate existing regional contrasts. Farm enlargement is most marked in eastern areas of arable farming, where farms are already large and economies of scale make it advantageous to acquire more land and so to use existing equipment and labour over larger areas. In the upland margins farms are small and the range of possible enterprises limited, but the government is now encouraging amalgamation by contributing towards the cost and pensions or grants for those who leave farming. Farmers are able to secure some of the economies of scale by cooperation and the number of business groups has risen sharply in recent years. Buyers of agricultural produce are also organized on a larger scale and retail food chains increasingly purchase direct from farmers. Much of the rising proportion of produce being processed is also grown on contract, as with peas for quick freezing; this development is only one of the many ways in which farming and industry are becoming interdependent.

Specialization by farm is accompanied by greater specialization by area. For most of the past hundred years regional trends in crop areas and livestock numbers have generally followed national patterns, but marked divergences have occurred since the mid-1950s. While the area under crops in eastern counties has been rising and now exceeds wartime levels, that in western counties continues to fall; by contrast, dairy cows are increasingly to be found in the western lowlands as arable farmers give up dairy herds and grazing livestock. Similarly, sheep are increasingly localized on the upland margins and there are other examples of greater regionalization.

Trends towards larger enterprises and greater specialization can be expected to continue and there will probably be some 10,000 fewer farms by 1975, and possibly 30,000 or 40,000 if a policy of farm amalgamation is vigorously pursued. Even if the United Kingdom does not enter the Common Market, the upward trend in the amount of land growing cereals is likely to persist, although the absence of further ploughable land in eastern counties and the problems posed by continuous cereal cropping suggest that the part played by other areas in lowland Britain will increase, as it has in the last decade.

The government is also likely to continue to encourage the production of beef, 30 per cent of which is still imported, but rising surpluses of milk will probably lead to a decline in the number of dairy cattle and their further concentration in western lowlands. Numbers of both pigs and broilers will continue to rise, but those of egg-laying fowl will not, although the abolition of the Egg Marketing Board should lead to a concentration of production nearer the major urban centres. Entry into the Common Market would provide a stronger stimulus to increase output of cereals and beef, but worsen the competitive position of dairy farmers and egg producers; at the same time, higher cereal prices would encourage the use of grass for livestock production.

Whatever the changes within the farming industry, agriculture's relations with other land uses will also alter. One certain feature is that the supply of agricultural land will continue to diminish. In the early 1960s, losses for houses, factories, roads and other 'site purposes' averaged 18,000 hectares a year, although this was a quarter less than in the 1930s; more than 4,000 hectares were taken for mineral working, though most will eventually be reclaimed. A further 24,000 hectares of agricultural land were converted into woodland each year, by private landowners and the Forestry Commission. Losses to urban development are inevitable if a rising population is to be housed and if the stock of slums and sub-standard houses is to be replaced; but such losses are irreversible, and involve land of above average quality. While the location of such transfers cannot greatly be altered, care must be taken, as it has been since the 1947 Town and Country Planning Acts, to ensure that good agricultural land is not used where this can be avoided.

The conversion of land from agriculture to forestry is neither inevitable nor irreversible; it is the result of policy decisions to expand home production of timber. The consequences of such losses are less serious, for the quality of land taken is generally well below average. Most planting occurs on the rough grazings of the lower hill-slopes of the west and north of Great Britain and, although afforestation can disrupt farming by separating high and low ground, it can also benefit hill farms by providing shelter. The Forestry Commission can acquire such land only with the consent of the agricultural departments; but no such restraints affect private afforestation and the scale of subsidized private planting has caused considerable alarm to farmers in recent years. In the absence of any long-term plan for forestry, the persistence of these trends is a matter of speculation, but the quality of the land transferred and the benefits that may accrue to the remaining farmland suggest that planting on the present scale need have no adverse effects on agriculture.

Even within the land areas nominally in agricultural use, other demands generated by the urban community have an increasing effect on agriculture. More people, rising standards of living, greater mobility and greater leisure lead to greater recreational use of the countryside, particularly in those areas of open rough grazing which are accessible from large cities. Intensive farming is made difficult on enclosed land in the lowlands, especially on the urban fringe, by pollution, trespass and vandalism. Attempts are being made to canalize such recreational pressures by the provision of country parks and picnic sites; in any case, all is not lost, for a crop of caravans is often the most profitable use of farmland.

The growing demand for water leads to the creation of new reservoirs, flooding valuable valleys in upland areas and often imposing restraints on the agricultural uses of catchments. Barrages and economic methods of desalination may remove this need in time, but not before new reservoirs become necessary. Military training, too, is likely to make further demands on agricultural land as overseas bases are abandoned. Agriculture in turn reacts on these and other uses. The increasing scale of farm operations, whether in the larger fields encouraged by mechanization or in the large buildings which house livestock or store crops, creates conflict with visual amenity, while uprooting hedges, reclaiming wild land and applying pesticides and herbicides create problems for the conservation of wild life.

How to achieve a more efficient agriculture and yet to maintain environmental quality and satisfy the legitimate requirements of other land users represents a major problem for British agriculture in the years ahead. Its solution is complicated by great regional differences in both the structure and the context of British farming. How can

4. *Every year new land is taken for housing, factories and roads. Although planning controls such as London's Green Belt help to prevent sprawl, further losses are inevitable. To add to the wastage, areas threatened with development are often neglected.*

a policy appropriate to the large, highly capitalized arable farms of eastern England be reconciled with that suitable for the small livestock farms of the upland margins which bring their occupiers less than a statutory agricultural wage?

How far should the Exchequer support the spare-time farmer, an increasingly common figure on the land around our great cities, farming for pleasure and deriving his main source of income from other employment? Where should amenity have priority over efficiency and how should farmers be compensated for any restraints imposed upon them? Both around the towns, where farming is increasingly handicapped by other pressures, and in areas of high landscape quality, which are often of less than average agriculture value, the farmer's role as the nation's gardener may well become as important as his contribution to food production. In other lowland areas, priorities will be reversed, although the problems of reconciling intensive agriculture with conservation remain unsolved and are of particular importance in those counties where large-scale arable farming is practised.

In the uplands, which contribute perhaps one-twentieth of agricultural output, though they occupy one-third of all land used for farming, problems are as much social as agricultural. For nearly a century run-down farmland and abandoned farmsteads have been features of these sparsely-populated areas, where farms are often too small and farmers elderly. Land improvement is technically possible, but the necessary capital would generally provide a better return if invested in lowland agriculture. Improving farm structure will help, but the best prospects lie in integrating farming into various systems of multiple land use.

In retrospect, the late 1960s may well appear as yet another watershed in the evolution of British farming. Much will depend on negotiations in Brussels* and on decisions on the desirable level of home food production, but agricultural policy will also have to be formulated in a wider context than hitherto. In a country where full-time farmers constitute less than one per cent of the working population, the urban majority must ask and answer, not only the question, 'What value do we place on home-grown produce?' but also 'What sort of countryside do we want and how much are we prepared to pay for it?'

References

Agriculture Adjustment Unit, *Farm Size Adjustment*, University of Newcastle, 1968.

Central Office of Information, *Agriculture in Britain*, 1969.

Cracknell, B. E., *Past and Future Cereals Production in the United Kingdom*, Home Grown Cereals Authority, 1970.

* See p. 166.

Davey, B. H., *Trends in Agriculture*, Agriculture Adjustment Unit, 1967.

Donaldson, J. G. S. and Frances, *Farming in Britain Today*, Allen Lane The Penguin Press, 1969.

Gasson, R., *The Influence of Urbanisation on Farm Ownership and Practice*, Studies in Rural Land Use, No. 7, Wye College, 1966.

Hinton, W. L., *Outlook for Horticulture*, Farm Economics Branch, University of Cambridge, 1968.

Ministry of Agriculture, Fisheries and Food, *Type of Farming Maps in England and Wales*, 1968.

Ministry of Agriculture, Fisheries and Food, and Department of Agriculture and Fisheries for Scotland, *A Century of Agricultural Statistics*, 1968.

Wibberley, G. P., *Agriculture and Urban Growth*, Michael Joseph, 1959.

New Directions for Transport

by Allan Patmore

Henry Booth, promoter and first historian of the pioneer Liverpool & Manchester Railway, wrote as the line was being completed: 'Speed–despatch–distance are still relative terms but their meaning has totally changed within a few months.' Railways – a new transport network embodying the universal application of mechanical traction – brought change indeed to the Britain of the 1830s: they became the arteries of an urban, industrial society and symbolized the technological and industrial pre-eminence of the 'workshop of the world'.

The withdrawal of the last steam locomotive in August 1968 symbolized the end of an era in more ways than one, for the 1960s were no less a watershed than the 1830s in transport development. Changes initiated in pre- or immediate post-war years came to fruition, new technologies emerged, new means of transport gained widespread acceptance. Other changes have been of degree rather than of kind, but with equally profound implications. Diesel traction and electrification on the railways, a proliferation of vehicles on the roads, gigantic bulk carriers and containers at sea, subsonic and jumbo jets in the air, mark the new technology; and with the new technology come transformed transport networks and terminals – shrinking railways, burgeoning motorways, deep-water oil terminals and container berths, lengthened runways and relocated airports.

The sum total of such change represents a colossal capital investment, not all of which yields a visible and direct return. London's new Victoria underground line cost some £70 million for the first sixteen kilometres of route and while it is expected to cover its operating expenses it will meet only part of the interest repayments on the capital borrowed to build it. With investment on this scale, government at local and national level is inevitably and intimately involved in determining the extent and direction of that investment. Transport projects can rarely be considered in isolation, whether in the private or public sectors: priorities must be judged in the light of political and social as well as economic criteria. Resulting decisions seldom find universal acceptance. Sir Donald Stokes sees road haulage 'bedevilled by politicians who seem to get industries, ideologies and ideas all inextricably intermingled'. But even in the heyday of Victorian *laissez-faire*, railway construction and operation was closely supervised (if not financed) by government agencies. It is perhaps as much a measure of public involvement as of the scale of change that the 1968 Transport Bill provoked 2,500 amendments to its 169 initial clauses and that its Committee stage, the longest of any Bill, filled 3,500 columns of *Hansard*.

It is not the purpose of this chapter to examine in detail the role of government planning or assess investment priorities in transport: rather the focus is on the implications of such planning and investment and the effects of changing technology on transport networks, and the impact of those networks on the wider economic and social patterns of the country.

Contraction provokes more hostility than expansion; this is certainly the case with Britain's railways. The Victorian legacy of railway monopoly was challenged between the wars, but not until the 1950s did railway finances really deteriorate. In 1961, faced with a mounting annual deficit (which was to reach almost £160 million by 1962), a Conservative government sought a commercial solution: Dr Beeching was brought from I.C.I. and appointed chairman with a clear mandate 'so to shape and operate the railways as to make them pay'. The Beeching Report of 1963 was a fundamental landmark, though its merits of positive thinking were obscured by bitter reaction to its proposals to close 55 per cent of existing track. As Michael Robbins has remarked, 'the railway was a thing people valued having, in its early days, and one they still value so long, very often, as other people will pay for it'. Closures were no new phenomenon: in the twelve years prior to the writing of the Beeching Report, passenger or freight services had been withdrawn from some 6,850 kilometres of route – though not all such withdrawals meant the complete closure to all traffic of the lines concerned. Since 1963 closures have accelerated. By 1970 less than 19,500 kilometres remained of a network which exceeded 31,000 kilometres at nationalization in 1948, and passenger services were only operated over some 15,000 kilometres (Figure 1).

Such pruning has eliminated duplicate routes spawned in the heat of railway competition, like that from Marylebone to Sheffield, and lines in rural and remote areas where road transport is a more flexible substitute. Nevertheless, many services remain which are still in a narrowly commercial sense unprofitable. These include suburban lines, where much rolling stock is utilized for only short periods each day, and many semi-fast stopping services. Recognizing the desirability and even the necessity in broader cost-benefit terms of retaining many of these services, the 1968 Transport Act provided an annual subsidy for 'socially desirable but unremunerative' passenger services. In 1970 this subsidy cost some £58 million, but the proportion of the existing network within this category is surprisingly large.

One by-product of closure has been the release of large tracts of land for other development. Property sales were worth £17 million to British Rail in 1968 and £14 million in 1969. Many were of disused yards and stations in urban areas which rapidly found alternative uses, but in rural areas, disposal and the prevention of visual deterioration is by no means so easy. Some stretches have become worthwhile footpaths; one in Cheshire is to be the nucleus of a country park, the Wirral Way.

Railways still have an effective part to play in their own right. In Britain, many passenger journeys between crowded cities are of a length where rail travel can compete effectively with both road and air. Indeed, only on Anglo-Scottish services has the impact of air competition been really serious. On the freight side, coal traffic, the long-term staple, has drastically declined but bulk movement in block trains of such commodities as oil, limestone, manufactured chemicals, cars and car components has increased. Improved handling methods allow more effective utilization of vehicles: the Freightliner network is moving increasing volumes of containerized general traffic after a hesitant start and 'merry-go-round' workings feed giant power stations with coal.

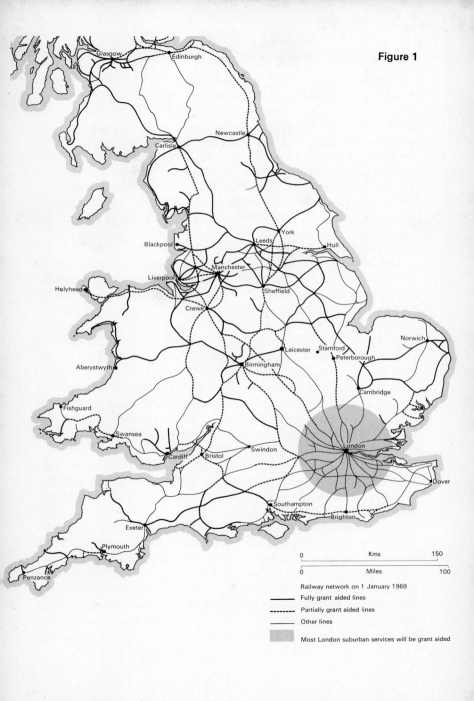

Figure 1

Glasgow

Edinburgh

Newcastle

Carlisle

Blackpool

Leeds York

Hull

Liverpool

Manchester

Holyhead

Sheffield

Crewe

Norwich

Leicester Stamford

Aberystwyth

Peterborough

Birmingham

Cambridge

Fishguard

Swansea

Swindon

Cardiff Bristol

London

Dover

Southampton

Exeter

Brighton

Plymouth

Penzance

| 0 | Kms | 150 |
| 0 | Miles | 100 |

Railway network on 1 January 1969

———— Fully grant aided lines

- - - - Partially grant aided lines

———— Other lines

Most London suburban services will be grant aided

For the railway, freed from common carrier obligations, the emphasis is essentially on trunk hauls between major centres, over routes shorn of the majority of intermediate traffic facilities. Where traffic flows are adequate, major investments are fully justified. The electrification from London to the West Midlands and Lancashire cost £160 million but has shown returns sufficient even on narrowly commercial grounds to support the case for its extension to Glasgow, an extension authorized in 1970. Work is well advanced on development of the Advanced Passenger Train, capable with gas turbine propulsion of speeds up to 240 k.p.h. while still using existing track and existing signalling. But the long-term railway-future of places like Aberystwyth or Aviemore must inevitably be in doubt.

The road has usurped the Victorian position of the railway as the universal carrier. The explosive growth in private and commercial vehicles needs no reiteration, totals rising from 3·5 million in 1947 to 14·8 million in 1969. Private vehicles were responsible for 75 per cent of all passenger kilometres in 1968 (as against 45 per cent in 1956): in the same year road transport carried 72,000 million ton-kilometres of freight, or 58 per cent of the total by all forms of transport. Increasing convenience in personal mobility and increasing freedom in industrial location, however, must be matched against increasing congestion. The problem in an urban setting requires a separate study of its special aspects, but in an inter-urban context a solution has been sought in the creation of an entirely new transport network, purpose-built for the motor age.

It is fascinating to see how successive transport networks pass through similar phases and repeat the same patterns. Railways followed canals, and borrowed their techniques of civil engineering and labour organization. After an initial phase of experimentation, the first major schemes sought to cater for trunk flows where traffic volumes were greatest. Proliferation followed in the 1840s as commercial success gave rise to a fever of speculation, and subsequently the most remote areas clamoured for the benefits of this form of communication. Now the motorway network follows suit. The M1 paralleled in its first section the London & Birmingham Railway of 1838 (Figures 2 and 3): in fact, the whole network of motorways in the early 1970s bears an uncanny resemblance to the railway network

RAILWAY MAP OF ENGLAND AND WALES
Shewing Railways opened to end of year 1844.

Railways opened in or before the year 1842
Railways opened in the year 1843 with day of opening.
Railways opened in the year 1844 with day of opening.
Railways sanctioned in or prior to 1843 and subsequently completed
Railways sanctioned in 1844

LIST OF PRINCIPAL RAILWAYS.

London and Birmingham
London and South Western
Edinburgh and Glasgow
Newcastle and Carlisle
Stockton and Darlington
Liverpool and Manchester
Taff Vale
Chester and Holyhead
Lancaster and Carlisle
Y. and N.M. — York and Scarboro'
E.C. — extension to Peterboro'
and Brandon
South Devon
Furness
Brighton, Lewes and Hastings
Eastern Union

Great Western
Bristol and Exeter
London and Brighton
York and North Midland
North British

Grand Junction
South Eastern
Northern and Eastern
Midland Counties
Hull and Selby
Glasgow and Greenock

Eastern Counties
Birmingham and Derby Junction
Manchester and Leeds
Glasgow, Paisley, Kilmarnock,
and Ayr
Bristol and Gloucester
North Wales Mineral
Brighton and Chichester

Great North of England
Newcastle and Darlington Junction
North Union
Birmingham and Gloucester
Preston and Wyre
Norwich and Brandon
Manchester, Bury, and Rossendale

Manchester and Birmingham
North Midland
Lancaster and Preston Junction
Chester and Birkenhead

0   Miles   60

Figure 2

MINISTRY OF TRANSPORT
MOTORWAY PROGRESS MAP

COMPLETED
UNDER CONSTRUCTION
LINE FIXED
SELECTION OF TRUNK ROADS ALSO
SHOWN IN THIN BLACK LINE

0   KILOMETRES   100
0   MILES   60

Figure 3

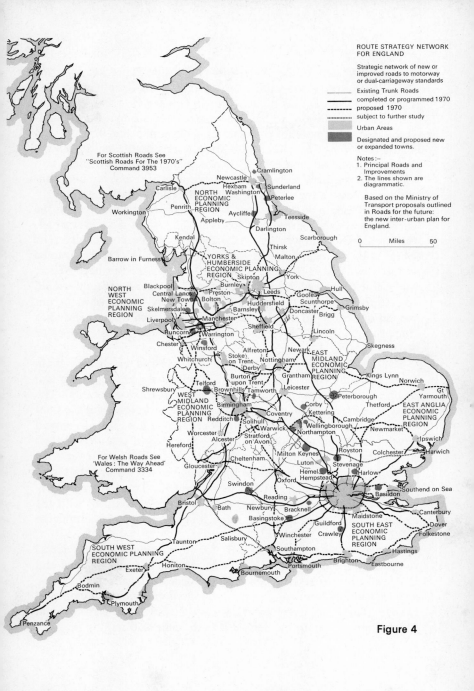

ROUTE STRATEGY NETWORK
FOR ENGLAND

Strategic network of new or
improved roads to motorway
or dual-carriageway standards

Existing Trunk Roads

completed or programmed 1970

proposed 1970

subject to further study

Urban Areas

Designated and proposed new
or expanded towns.

Notes :—
1. Principal Roads and
   Improvements
2. The lines shown are
   diagrammatic.

Based on the Ministry of
Transport proposals outlined
in Roads for the future:
the new inter-urban plan for
England.

0   Miles   50

For Scottish Roads See
"Scottish Roads For The 1970's"
Command 3953

Cramlington

Newcastle
Carlisle   Hexham
            Washington   Sunderland
Workington Penrith   Peterlee
NORTH
ECONOMIC
PLANNING
REGION   Aycliffe
            Appleby   Teesside
Kendal   Darlington

                              Scarborough
                        Thirsk
Barrow in Furness   Malton
            YORKS &
            HUMBERSIDE
            ECONOMIC PLANNING
            REGION
            Skipton   York
Blackpool   Burnley   Leeds   Hull
Central Lancs   Preston
NORTH   New Town   Bolton   Goole
WEST   Huddersfield   Scunthorpe
ECONOMIC Skelmersdale Barnsley Doncaster   Grimsby
PLANNING Liverpool   Manchester
REGION   Runcorn   Sheffield   Brigg
Chester Warrington   Lincoln
         Winsford   Alfreton
Whitchurch   Stoke   Nottingham Newark   Skegness
                  on Trent   EAST
                  Derby   MIDLAND
         Telford Burton   ECONOMIC Kings Lynn Norwich
Shrewsbury   upon Trent Grantham PLANNING
         WEST   Brownhills Tamworth Leicester REGION
         MIDLAND
         ECONOMIC Birmingham   Peterborough Gt
         PLANNING   Corby   Yarmouth
         REGION Redditch Solihull Kettering   Thetford EAST ANGLIA
Worcester   Coventry   Wellingborough Cambridge ECONOMIC
         Warwick   Northampton   Newmarket PLANNING
Hereford Alcester Stratford   REGION
                  on Avon Milton Keynes Royston   Ipswich
         Cheltenham   Luton Stevenage Colchester Harwich
For Welsh Roads See   Hemel   Harlow
'Wales : The Way Ahead' Gloucester Hempstead
Command 3334   Oxford   Basildon
                  Swindon   Southend on Sea
         Bristol   Reading
                  Bath Newbury Bracknell   Maidstone   Canterbury
                       Basingstoke   SOUTH EAST Dover
                            Guildford   ECONOMIC Folkestone
         Taunton   Salisbury Winchester Crawley PLANNING
                                          REGION Hastings
SOUTH WEST   Southampton
ECONOMIC PLANNING   Portsmouth Brighton Eastbourne
REGION   Honiton   Bournemouth
Exeter
Bodmin
Plymouth
Penzance

Figure 4

before the 'mania' of the 1840s, while the White Paper *Roads for the Future* (Ministry of Transport, 1970) foreshadows a proliferation not unrelated to subsequent railway growth (Figure 4).

As did the railways, so have the motorways brought a new landscape and new patterns of social and economic life. Bridges and viaducts of pre-stressed concrete are often as aesthetically pleasing in their functional simplicity as their stone and iron forbears. Bold swathes of six-lane highway are as familiar and as seemingly unobtrusive now as twin ribbons of iron were in an earlier era.

In their disdain of rural access, motorways are as withdrawn as the early railways, though existing roads are important secondary distributors. Equally, they bring a new focus to economic activity. The M1 is aptly dubbed the main street of Megalopolis. The M6 is to be the axis of Preston–Leyland–Chorley New Town: Burnley, Nelson and Colne could well feel as ill-served in relation to it as Stamford did to Peterborough in the railway age. Socially, motorways permit recreation seekers to travel much farther in a given time: the M6 has done for the Lake District what the railway did for Blackpool or Brighton.

But the motorway network and its envisaged extensions again focus development on a relatively concentrated area, repeating and at times even intensifying the patterns of an earlier generation. The road, admittedly, permits much looser concentrations than the tight urban agglomerations of the railway era, but it does little to spread development and overcome regional disparities of resource endowment. Major road construction projects annually absorb over £300 million, yet many schemes are on routes parallel to under-utilized railways. The licensing restrictions of the 1968 Transport Act foreshadowed a more calculated consideration of investment with the avowed intention of diverting more long-distance freight traffic to rail haulage.

Movement by sea and air calls for little expenditure on actual routes save for navigational aids, but changes in traffic volume and in size and type of vessel or aircraft have profoundly affected the scale and location of terminals. Ports are undergoing more fundamental changes than in any previous era, with capital investment rising from £18 million a year in the early 1960s to some £50 million in 1970.

5. Liverpool's Gladstone container terminal exemplifies the new landscape of the ·container port. Containers stacked on open ground for trans-shipment cover greater areas than the traditional transit shed.

The advent of giant bulk carriers of 250,000 deadweight tons and more has placed a premium on deep water, while the facility of pipeline movement for their cargo means that the ready availability of shore installations is less important than before. Milford Haven and Finnart exploit the deep water of natural but relatively isolated harbours, being linked by pipeline to Llandarcy and Grangemouth respectively. Perhaps the ultimate in this search for harbour rather than hinterland is in the development of the Bantry Bay terminal among the rias of south-west Ireland for the 317,000 ton tankers of the Gulf fleet.

Conversely, the development of containers has focused attention on shore facilities, but facilities very different from the traditional transit sheds and warehouse. The container itself has long been familiar – the principle being used on 18th-century canals – but did not come into widespread shipping use until the mid 1960s. Now, however, a container berth is a major status symbol for a port, and port authorities have tried to obtain the necessary government approval for large-scale developments embodying facilities for handling container traffic. At London, the £30 million Tilbury scheme was finished in 1969 giving thirteen new berths, six of them for container traffic. Liverpool's Seaforth project, costing some £40 million, is under construction, while Southampton's container facilities are being expanded at a cost of over £11 million.

Investment in airports is also a burning issue. Internal traffic is within the capacity of existing terminals until a later generation of vertical or short take-off and landing aircraft diverts more passengers to the air. London poses a very different problem. Heathrow handles more international traffic than any other airport in the world and, in value of cargo, is Britain's third largest port. Despite considerable capital investment (£11·4 million in 1968/9 and £9·5 million in 1969/70), it is now nearing its effective capacity and, even with the growing use of Gatwick, will need to be supplemented by further airport capacity in the 1970s. The Roskill Commission's recommendation of Cublington as the site for a third London airport was turned down by the government in April 1971 in favour of Foulness. However, it is an indication of the increasing efficiency of ground transport as well as the shortage of land that all four sites in the short list considered by the Commission were in the order of sixty kilometres or further from the centre of London.

The scale of capital investment in the creation of transport facilities and the degree of government involvement in their planning need constant emphasis; this applies equally to other forms of transport such as inland waterways, pipelines and the whole field of telecommunications. Paradoxically, advancing technology frequently limits rather than extends transport availability in areal terms, with emphasis on fewer units of greater capacity but less flexibility. The simple airports which ringed London before the war yield to the complexity of Heathrow and Gatwick, and numerous trunk roads to a single motorway. The choice of location (and the avoidance of duplication) therefore assumes ever greater importance and gives the government powers of positive planning unrivalled in any other field, for investment affects not only the transport form itself but the whole of the economic and social activities which it generates and sustains. Regional development and regional distinction are seemingly nurtured or stifled with appalling ease. Technology may decide what *can* be done but it rarely decides what *will*: humane planning, aware not only of cost-benefit and economic return but also of the geographical reality of amenity and tradition, is vitally necessary if quality as well as efficiency of living is to be sustained.

References

Allen, G. F., *British Rail after Beeching*, Ian Allan, 1966.

Annual Reports of British Railways Board, British Waterways Board, British Airports Authority; annual issues of *Roads in England & Wales* (Ministry of Transport), HMSO.

Appleton, J. H., *The Geography of Communications in Great Britain*, OUP, 1962.

Bird, J. H., *The Major Seaports of the United Kingdom*, Hutchinson, 1963.

British Waterways Board, *The Facts about the Waterways*, 1965.

Drake, J., Yeadon, H. L., and Evans, D. I., *Motorways*, Faber & Faber, 1970.

Ministry of Transport, *Roads for the Future: the New Inter-Urban Plan for England*, Cmnd 4369, HMSO, 1970.

Sealy, K. R., *The Geography of Air Transport*, Hutchinson, 2nd edition, 1966.

The Proper Place for Industry

by David Keeble

As the dreary succession of post-war balance of payments crises has re-emphasized time and again, the United Kingdom, the 19th-century 'workshop of the world', is still vitally dependent for its prosperity upon its manufacturing industries. From a geographical viewpoint, this suggests that if the country is to pay its way abroad, its manufacturing firms must be encouraged to grow and develop in those locations which offer the greatest opportunities for maximizing the efficiency and minimizing the costs of production. Put another way, investment, especially in key modern industries, must be intimately related geographically to the pattern of Britain's resources for industrial growth, so that these may be harnessed to the full in the struggle for maximum industrial efficiency and exports.

In reality, however, the geography of industrial investment in the United Kingdom today appears to be the product of two largely separate sets of locational forces, in turn related to different industrial resources. One is the force of natural, 'free market', growth of private industry, influencing industrial location patterns by different rates of expansion or decline in different regions. The other is the force of government industrial location policy, influencing the geography of industrial investment by the sponsorship of actual movement of manufacturing firms from richer to poorer regions. Both sets need to be considered here.

Many post-war observers have viewed the national pattern of recent 'natural' industrial development in terms of a north–south division, into industrially-lagging and industrially-growing regions. Phrases such as 'the drift to the south' and 'the north begins at Watford' have become part of national folklore. Yet as Caesar (1964) has powerfully argued, recent British industrial growth is almost certainly more realistically viewed in terms, not of a north–

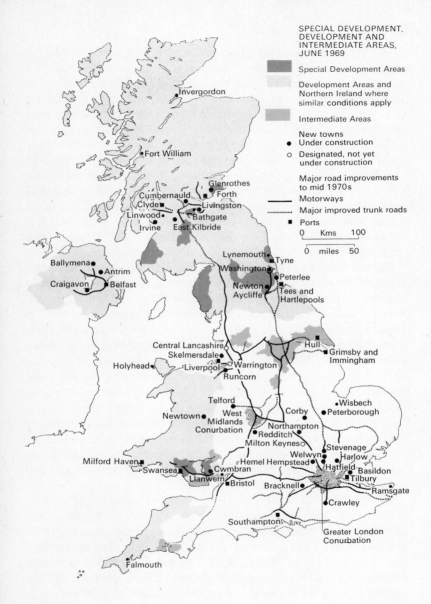

SPECIAL DEVELOPMENT,
DEVELOPMENT AND
INTERMEDIATE AREAS,
JUNE 1969

Special Development Areas

Development Areas and
Northern Ireland where
similar conditions apply

Intermediate Areas

New towns
● Under construction
○ Designated, not yet
  under construction

Major road improvements
to mid 1970s
── Motorways
····· Major improved trunk roads
■ Ports

0   Kms   100

0   miles   50

Invergordon

Fort William

Glenrothes
Cumbernauld   Forth
Clyde   Livingston
Linwood   Bathgate
Irvine   East Kilbride

Ballymena   Antrim
Craigavon   Belfast

Lynemouth   Tyne
Washington   Peterlee
Newton   Tees and
Aycliffe   Hartlepools

Central Lancashire
Skelmersdale   Hull   Grimsby and
Holyhead   Liverpool   Warrington   Immingham
            Runcorn

Telford   Corby   Wisbech
Newtown   West   Peterborough
         Midlands   Northampton
         Conurbation   Redditch
              Milton Keynes   Stevenage
              Welwyn   Harlow
Milford Haven   Hemel Hempstead   Hatfield   Basildon
Swansea   Cwmbran   Tilbury
         Llanwern Bristol   Bracknell   Ramsgate
                        Crawley
              Southampton

                        Greater London
                        Conurbation

Falmouth

Figure 1

south, but of a centre–periphery pattern. The central industrially-expanding zone of the country, focused on the great urban-industrial nodes of London and Birmingham, stretches out to include much of South-east England, the East and West Midlands, and the Bristol area. Around it lie the less fortunate areas, characterized by higher than average unemployment and more sluggishly-growing or declining manufacturing industries (Figure 1). Though most readily apparent to the west (Wales) and the north (North-east England, the Lancashire textile towns, Cumberland, Scotland and Northern Ireland), the less fortunate periphery also includes parts of coastal and rural East Anglia and east Kent as well as the most southerly of all Britain's regions, Cornwall and Devon. Wisbech, Ramsgate and Falmouth, for example, have all had average unemployment rates double the national figure in recent years or even higher.

Natural 'free market' industrial growth in the central zone undoubtedly owes much to the centre's three major resources – position in relation to customers and suppliers, workers, and entrepreneurs. A recent study by Sant (1967) has shown that 'market potential', a measure of the nearness of a given point to United Kingdom markets for manufactured goods in terms of retail sales, declines in all directions from just this central zone of industrial growth. Wales, the south-west peninsula, east Kent, and North-east England, all have potential values less than 60 per cent of the London figure. Moreover, this is true even without taking account of the concentration of first-class road communications within this central zone, a concentration which makes it far easier for an industrialist in Dunstable to reach his customers quickly than for his Dundee competitor. Ease and cheapness of access to the national market has thus almost certainly aided the growth of centrally-located firms.

So too have the range of skills and the quantity of labour available in this, the country's most densely-populated zone. Surprisingly enough, in absolute rather than percentage terms, there are usually more unemployed workers available in Greater London than in the whole of Wales: while Census of Production evidence suggests that labour productivity in manufacturing may well be significantly higher in London than in most other parts of the country. The concentration of really skilled research scientists, technolo-

6. *In the East End of London small furniture, clothing and engineering factories operate in cramped conditions, cheek by jowl with houses and shops. Traffic and parking congestion aggravate labour shortages and resultant industrial emigration largely explains the colossal decline of 100,000 manufacturing jobs in inner London between 1961 and 1966.*

gists and managers in South-east England, too, is now a well-established social phenomenon, of great economic significance to industry.

Most difficult to evaluate, but probably of crucial importance for industrial growth in the centre, is the role of its entrepreneurial resources. Though statistical evidence is limited, it is generally thought that the West Midlands and London are characterized by high industrial birth rates, small 'back-room' firms constantly springing up to exploit new markets, techniques or products. This 'nursery' function is certainly suggested by the remarkable number of migrant factories contributed by these two conurbations to other areas since the war: 1,500 factories or 56 per cent of the total UK moves recorded by the Board of Trade. If true, these high birth rates are almost certainly linked to the concentration of potential entrepreneurs in these areas. Skilled workers keen to have a go on their own, individual scientists with new ideas, foreign refugees with imported 'know-how', all seem to find in areas like South-east England the right environment for setting up their own infant manufacturing firms. The role of refugees in Britain's industrial growth in particular is one which seems to have escaped the attention it deserves. In one recent survey in London, over 10 per cent of a large random sample of manufacturing firms were found to have been set up by foreign immigrants, many of whom were uprooted from Europe by Nazi hostility or Communist takeover.

Technological change, moreover, is steadily enhancing the value of just these centrally-located resources. For example, increasingly complex technology is producing a greater dependence upon highly qualified scientific and managerial staff – who tend to be more easily available in central locations. Again, technological development seems to be creating more and more assembly-type industries, ranging from Concorde to deaf aids, which prefer central locations easily accessible to supporting component manufacturers. A third example concerns technologically advanced communication facilities, such as the proposed third London airport, the new mechanized container handling docks at Tilbury, British Rail's freightliner terminals as at Stratford and Willesden in London, and the recently electrified Euston–Manchester and Waterloo–Bournemouth rail links. All these, for reasons of cost and demand, tend to be at or between relatively few, centrally-located points, thereby enhancing the many advantages to industry of the central zone's positional resources.

Of course, the industrial geography of the centre is itself by no means static or uniform. For example, probably the most striking single change in Britain's industrial geography since the war has been the remarkable explosion of manufacturing firms outwards but within the centre, from its two great nodes of London and Birmingham to surrounding towns. Prompted by factory shortages and costs and by labour scarcity, this 'flight from the metropolis' has led to enormous manufacturing growth around London (represented by over 400,000 new manufacturing workers between 1951 and 1966) and, to a lesser extent, Birmingham, coupled with some apparent decline in manufacturing within these conurbations. Especially in the South-east, the centre's new towns have provided attractive locations for a number of these expanding migrant firms (Figure 2). On the national scale, a further change since 1945 is the extension, again largely through industrial migration, of the central growth zone's

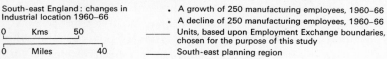

South-east England: changes in Industrial location 1960–66

0 Kms 50

0 Miles 40

. A growth of 250 manufacturing employees, 1960–66

∘ A decline of 250 manufacturing employees, 1960–66

_____ Units, based upon Employment Exchange boundaries, chosen for the purpose of this study

_____ South-east planning region

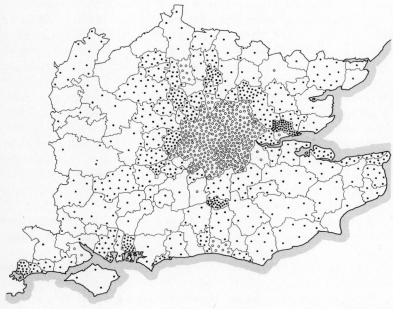

Figure 2

outer boundary to include new areas. Parts of East Anglia have certainly benefited in this way. Some observers also see eastern South Wales (now linked to the 'mainland' near Bristol by the Severn Bridge) and parts of North-west England (notably Merseyside) as having been drawn into the central growth belt since the war, as a result of colonization by expanding firms attracted from the Midlands and South-east England.

From the point of view of free market trends, the obverse side of the coin to a growing industrial centre is, of course, a declining or sluggishly-expanding industrial periphery. Geographically, in fact, the so-called 'regional problem' is fundamentally a peripheral problem. Most of the accepted indices of economic ill-health – percentage unemployment, rates of net out-migration of population, employment participation levels, even income per head – tend to form roughly concentric circles about the central growth zone. This tendency has led to what might be called the structural versus locational explanation controversy. Put simply, the structural school of thought argues that the economic problems of peripheral regions are due basically to over-specialization before 1900 on industries in which the demand for their products has declined, relatively or absolutely, in this century. Obvious examples are coalmining, iron and steel, shipbuilding, textiles and agriculture. In turn, this over-specialization at the periphery partly reflected the historical accident that many British coalfields, the industrial boom centres of the 19th century, happened to be located on or near the coast. The locational school, on the other hand, argues that although the historical legacy is obviously important, the basic reason for the relative economic distress of the periphery lies in its inability to attract spontaneously 20th-century growth industry: and that the main reason for this is the very fact of its peripheral nature, and resultant greater distance from customers and suppliers within Britain.

The importance of this controversy lies in the implicit but different policy conclusions involved. While acknowledging the psychological disadvantage of an historical legacy of slag-heaps, slums and derelict mills in attracting new industry, the structural viewpoint suggests that there is no inherent locational reason why new plants, once attracted by government policy, should not operate every bit as efficiently in the periphery as in the centre. The locational viewpoint, on the other hand, implies that there are sound economic reasons for the reluctance of newer industries to move to the periphery, in the shape of increased long-term costs of manufacturing and marketing: and that the steering of industry to peripheral areas may therefore result in a high-cost and economically undesirable industrial location pattern.

Whichever explanation may be nearer the truth, it would be grossly misleading to ignore the fact that, despite their unattractiveness to some modern industries, the peripheral areas do today possess significant resources which have attracted important industrial projects. Most obvious is the traditional raw material, coal. Nearby coal deposits help to explain the choice in 1959 of the Welsh village of Llanwern as the 'greenfield' site for Britain's biggest-ever single industrial development scheme – an entirely new £150,000,000 integrated iron and steel plant. Another, though less important, material resource is softwood timber. That found in the Scottish Highlands now feeds the mammoth Fort William pulp and paper mill. However, the most significant modern resources of the periphery are not materials, in the traditional, 19th-century sense, at all. Rather, as with the central areas, they are positional and human.

Paradoxically, the very peripheral character of areas such as Wales or Scotland confers upon certain locations within them the increasing advantage of deep-water access to imported foreign materials. With the remarkable technological development of huge crude oil and mineral ore carriers, the periphery's natural deep-water harbours are becoming increasingly attractive as 'break-of-bulk' locations for the burgeoning oil-refining and petro-chemical industries, and for other capital-intensive mineral-processing plants. The recent establishment of three big oil refineries (and a fourth scheduled to be built by 1973) on the lovely shores of Pembrokeshire's Milford Haven, with its sheltered and deepened anchorage for 274,000-ton tankers, illustrates both this trend and the 'jobs-versus-conservation' planning dilemma which it often poses. Even more striking is the recent choice of Holyhead, Lynemouth (Northumberland), and Invergordon (Scotland) as the coastal sites for three massive aluminium smelters, costing together over £140,000,000, which will process alumina shipped from as far afield as Australia and Jamaica.

The existing and potential human resources of the periphery, on the other hand, have become important through changes not in technology but in the overall national employment situation. Frequent post-war labour shortages in Greater London and the West Midlands, a product of the government's 'full employment' policy, have directed the attention of some centrally-located firms employing large numbers of semi-skilled workers to peripheral pools of unemployed and, more important, under-employed labour. The resultant establishment of branch factories in peripheral areas by firms with household names such as Glaxo, Hoover and Ronson is therefore in part at least 'natural' rather than government-sponsored migration. A special case is labour-orientated movement to Cornwall and Devon, where labour resources are potential rather than actual. The attractive holiday environment and 'image' of this area seem to be viewed by some immigrant firms as bait to attract skilled workers from central areas.

For much of the post-war period, then, the centre–periphery contrast in industrial development has been perpetuated by 'natural' trends, relating to the rather different resource endowments of the two zones. However, today, as in the immediate post-war years, the force of government industrial location policy is operating very powerfully to offset 'natural' trends, and encourage peripheral industrial investment. While basically motivated by social and political considerations, this policy stresses the economic importance of utilizing underemployed peripheral labour resources and damping down inflationary wage/price increases in the centre.

Government legislation to aid industrial development in the periphery, though dating back to the 1934 Special Areas Act, only became really effective in 1945, with the passing of the first Distribution of Industry Act. In this, and the whole gamut of subsequent location policy legislation, were embodied both negative powers to refuse permission for new factories in South-east England and the West Midlands, and positive inducements to peripheral industrial migration and development, largely in the form of advance factories, government-sponsored industrial estates and limited financial aid.

These powers enabled the then Labour government to seize the once-for-all opportunity of insatiable consumer demand and rocketing production levels provided by the post-war boom years to direct industry to peripheral locations. During the years 1945–9, nearly 400 migrant factories were established in the peripheral zone. However, with the onset of more normal economic conditions and of Conservative governments in the 1950s, location policy was not enforced so strictly.

This situation obtained very largely until about 1960, when a new period of strong government influence on industrial location was ushered in by the remarkable success of the Conservative government in persuading the country's five leading vehicle manufacturers to set up major car or lorry assembly plants actually in peripheral regions – three on Merseyside (Ford, Vauxhall and Standard-Triumph) and

7. *When Ford Motor Company decided in* 1960 *to build a plant at Halewood, it marked a breakthrough in post-war government regional development policy. Ford's Merseyside factories now represent an £80,000,000 investment.*

two in Scotland (Rootes at Linwood and B.M.C. at Bathgate). However, it took yet another Labour government, gaining power in 1964, radically to increase financial incentives to industrial location

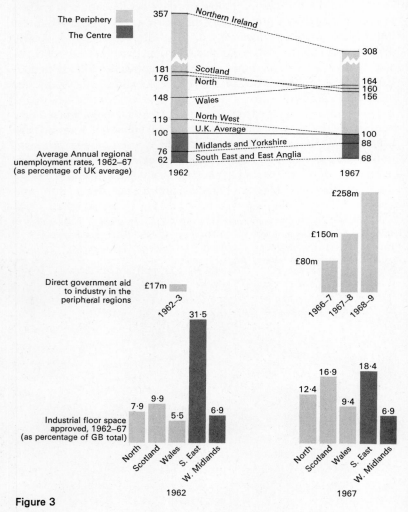

Figure 3

at the periphery. The institution of a Regional Employment Premium and establishment of a differential in the payment of Selective Employment Tax, coupled with the payment of investment grants on new plant and machinery double those outside the present Development Areas, boosted direct subsidies and grants to peripheral industry from under £20,000,000 in 1962–3 to no less than an estimated £258,000,000 in 1968–9 (Figure 3).

The result of these colossal incentives and of post-1960 government action generally has been a marked improvement, at least until recently, in the rate of industrial development in the peripheral regions. Unemployment percentages, except in Wales, have fallen relative to the national average: while the periphery's proportion of new factory space approved by the Board of Trade has risen dramatically. Industrial restructuring has thus reached a point where new industries, such as electronics in Scotland, often now employ more workers than the old staples, such as coalmining.

Yet the apparent recent success of government policy raises further problems. Is the massive cost of the policy economically justifiable in the long term? The Linwood car assembly plant, symbol of Scotland's industrial regeneration, was still not making a profit in 1969, after six years of operation. Is it right to regard Greater London as an inexhaustible source of migrant firms? Or may its capacity to generate new virile industry be damaged by continuing curbs on industrial expansion, as both the Greater London Council and the Hunt Committee seem to think? What too of the economic problems of the 'intermediate' or 'grey' areas, lying at the junction of centre and periphery, especially with the virtual rejection of the Hunt Committee's recommendations? Will a mere £14 million a year of government aid for factory building and land clearance be sufficient to encourage successful long-term industrial growth? Is the total supply of mobile industry sufficient to meet simultaneously the needs of the centre's ambitious overspill programme (South East Joint Planning Team, 1970), with entirely new cities like Milton Keynes, and those of the periphery? Lastly, is the disturbing recent (1971) fall in the share of factory approvals going to peripheral regions a direct result of the October 1970 changes in location incentives decreed by the new Conservative government (involving the.

promised abolition of REP by 1974, and the replacement of investment grants by tax allowances)? Or is it simply a temporary setback, caused by earlier deflationary measures? The government's answers to these questions could have a profound effect not just on the geography of future industrial investment, but on the long-term industrial efficiency and economic prosperity of the United Kingdom as a whole.

References

Caesar, A. A. L., 'Planning and the Geography of Great Britain', *Advancement of Science*, 21, no. 91, pp. 230–40, 1964.

Cameron, G. C., and Clark, B. D., *Industrial Movement and the Regional Problem*, University of Glasgow, Social and Economic Studies, Occasional Papers, 5, 1966.

Clark, C., 'Industrial Location and Economic Potential', *Lloyds Bank Review*, 82, pp. 1–17, 1966.

Keeble, D. E., 'Industrial Decentralization and the Metropolis: the North-West London Case', *Transactions of the Institute of British Geographers*, 44, pp. 1–54, 1968.

Manners, G., 'Areas of Economic Stress: the British Case', pp. 139–64 in W. D. Wood & R. S. Thoman (eds.), *Areas of Economic Stress in Canada*, Queen's University, Kingston, Ontario, 1965.

McCrone, G., *Regional Policy in Britain*, 15, Allen & Unwin, London, 1969.

Sant, M. E. C., 'Unemployment and Industrial Structure in Great Britain', *Regional Studies*, 1, 1, pp. 83–91, 1967.

South East Joint Planning Team, *Strategic Plan for the South East*, HMSO, 1970.

Warren, K., *The British Iron and Sheet Steel Industry since 1840*, Bell, 1970.

Energy and Problems in Abundance

by Gerald Manners

Behind those skilful advertising campaigns for 'High Speed Gas', white electricity meters, oil-fired central heating and Approved Coal Merchants lies an increasingly competitive market for energy. In part this is a response to the recent arrival of nuclear power and natural gas, transforming the base of the British energy economy from two fuels – coal and oil, just over a decade ago – into the four fuels of today. In part, it is the child of the increasing efficiency with which energy can be won and made available where it is required.

Measured in real terms, the costs of winning coal, of obtaining crude oil, of tapping supplies of natural gas and, of generating electricity have steadily fallen in recent years. The productivity of coal mining, for example, has been increased considerably by long-wall coalface machinery, by power loading and by use of powered supports. New low cost oil fields have been discovered and exploited in many parts of the world, to push potential supplies well in excess of world demand, and thus to cause a downward drift of market prices during the nineteen sixties. Technological advances have permitted the economical exploitation of offshore natural gas deposits, and brought about the prospective cessation of the much higher cost of manufacture of town gas from coal. And the generating sets of both conventional and nuclear power stations have become both larger and more efficient.

Great cost-reducing strides have also been made in transporting energy from its sources to where it is required – and it is in the market that energy prices ultimately matter most. With the merry-go-round trains introduced between the pithead and power station; with super-tankers of 200,000 tons dead-weight and over steaming between the Gulf and our deepest estuaries; with a large diameter pipeline transmission system linking the North Sea terminals with the high pressure distribution systems of the area gas boards; and with the super-imposition of the 400 kV grid upon the existing 275 kV system for the transfer and the security of electrical energy supplies; the story is universally the same. All the energy industries are seeking to exploit larger units of equipment and more efficient means of transport in order to obtain lower unit costs and enhance their competitive positions.

There are, of course, differences in the degree of progress achieved by the competing producer-supplier industries. The electricity and gas industries have the considerable advantage of a fully integrated production and supply system. They produce or purchase their respective types of energy, and then transport and distribute it by means of a network of either wires or pipelines over which they have full control. The operation, modification, extension or contraction of their respective systems is entirely in their own hands. Improvements to the efficiency of the whole can be studied, judged and implemented without significant reference to outside bodies. Although the oil industry does not have the same utility-like qualities, and its market is shared between a number of companies, it too can boast a fairly well-integrated production-supply system, having part or total ownership of producing fields, crude pipelines, ocean bulk tankers, refineries, coastal tankers, product pipelines and road distribution vehicles. Only in the case of products transported by rail is there an element in the production-supply system which is not powerfully controlled by the industry itself. Yet even in this case the rail wagons, now carrying up to 100 tons each, are owned by the industry; and the quality of service offered by British Rail can be closely measured against alternative means of transport, especially pipelines.

The coal industry, in contrast, is characterized by a much more fragmented production-supply system. Beyond the pithead, many coal movements are outside the sole responsibility and control of the National Coal Board. Some are, of course, and the road distribution of coal in the Board's lorries, for example, is extremely efficient. Other coal transfers are jointly the responsibility of several parties, including the Board; an example is the railing of coal to the power stations of the Central Electricity Generating Board, optimized with the assistance of linear programming techniques – although the largest

8. Streamlined transport methods help to reduce costs of power supplies. Trainloads of coal can be automatically unloaded and conveyed to the stockpile at a rate of 1000 tons per hour using the merry-go-round tracks at the new 1,500 MW Aberthaw 'B' power station.

wagons remain only 32 tons. A large share of coal transport and distribution is in the hands of distributors and merchants, making use of the services of British Rail. These flows blatantly lack the scale and the efficiency required to compete in the energy markets of today. The National Coal Board has been trying to influence and control the transfer of more coal further down the supply system, encouraging rationalization and entering more openly into marketing operations. Yet the traditions, customs and habits of the past die hard – as well as imposing their costs – and the coal industry remains saddled with a comparatively unattractive set of supply arrangements.

Nevertheless, increasingly competitive bidding in the industrial fuel sector of the energy market has resulted in successes for each of the principal industries. In 1968–9, for example, the oil industry won a large British Steel Corporation contract, reputedly fixed at 2·1 p per therm. In converting to natural gas the Gas Council quickly won a series of major industrial contracts in the Potteries and West Midlands, as well as a major 15 year contract with Imperial Chemical Industries valued at 1·7 p per therm and totalling some £250 million. The National Coal Board secured a contract with Associated Portland Cement at under 1·7 p per therm, and later agreed to supply the new Northumberland smelter of Alcan at a pithead price of just over one penny per therm. Such agreements for the supply of bulk industrial fuels command the headlines in the industrial and financial press. These figures compare with the average price of gas sales to industry of 6·7 p.

No less important is the competition in many of the other sectors of the economy, which expresses itself ultimately in the substitution of one fuel for another. This has proceeded apace. In 1950, nearly 90 per cent of the inland market for 230 million tons of coal equivalent energy was provided by the coal mines of this country, and the rest – a small 0·4 per cent coming from hydro-electricity sites –

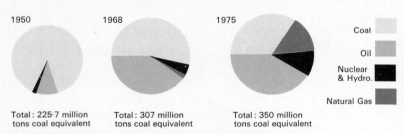

Figure 1   Changing patterns of primary fuel consumption.

was supplied by the oil industry. By 1969, out of a market for nearly 323 million tons of coal equivalent energy, coal satisfied 50·7 per cent, oil 42·7 per cent, nuclear and hydro-power about 4 per cent, and the first supplies of natural gas the rest (Figure 1). 1970–71 saw oil overhaul coal as the country's major fuel.

All the indicators suggest that these trends will continue. Notwith-

Figure 2   Overabundance of oil producing capacity has led to a steady fall in real prices. Refined products from Shell's 6 million ton oil refinery at Teesport are distributed to northern England and Scotland by road, rail and coastal tanker. The port takes fully laden vessels up to 85,000 tons dead-weight.

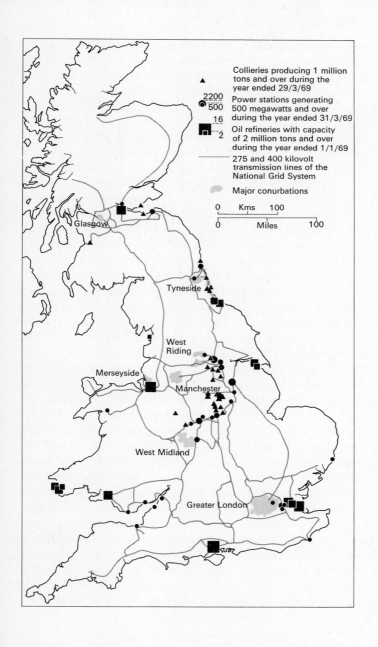

Colleries producing 1 million tons and over during the year ended 29/3/69

Power stations generating 500 megawatts and over during the year ended 31/3/69

$\frac{16}{-2}$ Oil refineries with capacity of 2 million tons and over during the year ended 1/1/69

275 and 400 kilovolt transmission lines of the National Grid System

Major conurbations

0   Kms   100

0   Miles   100

Glasgow

Tyneside

West Riding

Merseyside

Manchester

West Midland

Greater London

standing the recent increases in posted prices and taxes, it would be a bold observer of the international oil scene who predicted medium-term rises in (real) crude oil prices in a world of abundant supplies. Moreover, the oil industry can obviously reap further economies through the use of yet larger tankers, refineries and distribution systems. With the first North Sea gas contracts settled for 2·1 p per therm, and the more recent larger ones at 1·2 p per therm at a 60 per cent load factor, and 0·8 p at higher load factors, a beach price of around 1·0 p per therm would seem to be feasible in any large future purchases by the Gas Council. Lord Robens has claimed that a 9 to 10 per cent per annum increase in the productivity of the coal industry is within its reach, a claim substantiated by the fact that British mining machinery used in the United States is made to yield four times the output per manshift obtained in the best British mines. Conventional power stations have every prospect of being built larger, with a consequent reduction in real unit costs; and, although nuclear power will doubtless continue to disappoint its most fervent supporters, there can be no doubt that there is a firm downward trend in construction and total costs (Figure 3). The last of the first generation Magnox reactors, completed in 1971, will generate electricity at perhaps 0·29 p per kWh, compared with the first station at Berkeley (1962) where the costs were 0·51 p, and the prospect of 0·22 p at Hartlepool in 1974. With costs and prices of energy likely to move downwards in real terms in the foreseeable future, the substitution of one fuel for another is unlikely to abate.

To anticipate further competition and change in the British market for energy in purely qualitative terms is, however, insufficient for governments of today. This is an area of economic activity which is only too obviously of major public interest. Quite apart from the fact that, with the exception of the oil industry, this is a nationalized sector of the economy which used £845 million of new investment in 1969–70, certain political decisions cannot be evaded. The nuclear power industry and its future is impossible to conceive outside a politically defined framework; with its origins in a military decision to reach for an independent deterrent, nurtured by a huge public research investment, and historically subjected to innumerable government inquiries, reports, and policies, this is inevitably so.

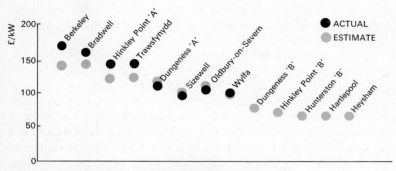

Figure 3   Nuclear power station construction costs

Again, concessions for the exploration of the continental shelf – and the determination of royalties if gas or oil are extracted – are legally the prerogative of the Minister of Power, whose department has been intimately concerned with the negotiation of the beach price of natural gas in recent years. The gradual contraction of coal production, and the even faster run-down of the mining labour force, present problems not only to the industry but also to those village and regional communities within which the coal industry is localized. Policy making cannot be indifferent to such matters, nor to the oil industry's huge investment abroad and the security issues which increasing imports raise at home.

It is perfectly possible for an administration to react to each energy industry piecemeal, responding to its immediate needs, pressures and opportunities. Successive governments did so until 1965. Since then, however, an attempt has been made to look at the energy sector of the economy as a whole, to recognize and reconcile conflicts in public attitudes, and to spell out a consistent fuel policy. The starting point for policy formulation is to assume that the preferences of the market place are paramount and patterns of energy use in target years are forecast on this basis. The strategic, economic and social implications of these trends and prospects are then noted and the desirability of public action considered. Following its 1967 White Paper, for example, the Government decided to pay the Central

Electricity Generating Board for burning coal which on commercial grounds it would not otherwise have used; funds were also made available to ameliorate the worst social effects of the National Coal Board's mine closure programme.

The most recent published forecasts of the Ministry of Power for the pattern of fuel use in 1975 still remain those of April 1967. Out of a total inland consumption of some 356 million tons of coal equivalent energy in the latter year the largest share, it is suggested, will be provided by oil – nearly 42 per cent. (Note that this proportion had already been exceeded in 1969.) Natural gas, it was forecast, will provide 14 per cent. Nuclear power and a dash of hydro-electricity will contribute rather less than 11 per cent. The share of the coal

9. Generating stations grow in size and efficiency. Didcot power station will be commissioned in 1972 to meet demand in southern England. More than 18,000 tons of coal and more than 225 million litres of water will be used daily to feed a capacity of 2,000 MW.

industry will have fallen to about 34 per cent (Figure 1). The political implications of a continuing decline of coal output to 125 million tons in 1975 compared with 182 million tons ten years earlier were such as to cause the Government to withdraw the 1967 White Paper for further study, following the devaluation of sterling. It was not subsequently re-presented to Parliament, although all the evidence suggests that it continues to provide the framework for many public policy decisions.

The adoption of an articulate fuel policy calls not only for boldness but also for flexibility. In the 1965 White Paper the forecast for 1970 coal production was 183 million tons; two years later, once the magnitude of the North Sea gas finds had been better established, this figure was revised downwards by 30 million tons. Such a contrast does not invalidate the exercise, but it reminds us that any forecasting technique must rest upon a series of assumptions concerning national economic growth, technical change, differential trends in fuel costs, industry pricing policies and the like. These are matters which cannot be determined in advance with accuracy, and a speculative element must of necessity permeate any government statement on fuel policy.

Thus, although there is political commitment to a minimum nuclear power programme in the nineteen seventies, the speed at which stations are ordered and built will undoubtedly be influenced by improvements in the technology and costs of the Advanced Gas Cooled reactor. No one doubts the ability of the gas industry to double its 1968 sales by 1970–71 to 25 million coal equivalent tons; but whether this can be doubled again by 1975 without entering the market for generating base and middle load electricity is a much more open question. In recent years the oil industry has been expanding its sales at an annual rate of 9 to 10 per cent. Government forecasts assume that some of this growth will be captured by the gas industry in the early nineteen seventies. Perhaps so; but it must be questioned whether the oil industry, which has the enormous advantage of large non-competitive markets (motor and aviation fuels), flexible pricing policies, a geographical scatter of production facilities and hence relatively low distribution costs, and a growing number of internationally-owned participants, is likely to let such a challenge go unanswered.

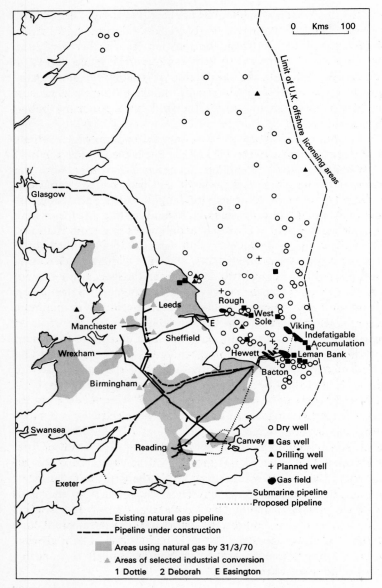

Figure 4

Undoubtedly the most acute uncertainties in British energy policy overhang the future of the coal industry. Even given the protection of a tax at £1·96 per ton on oil, doubts remain as to whether it can reduce its real unit costs in the wake of wage inflation and improve the efficiency of its distribution system sufficiently to retain a market of 120 million tons in 1975. How can the industry be given greater output flexibility and be made capable of responding to unexpected upswings in demand, such as occurred in 1970 and 1971? Will the ban on imports, lifted in 1970, have to be re-imposed? If the coal industry's production should shrink faster than forecast – it was down to just over 145 million tons in 1970 – can the industry possibly maintain the morale of the remaining labour force? Is there any validity in Lord Robens' claim that the contraction of mining employment must not be allowed to exceed 10 per cent of that workforce each year? Is the rate at which alternative employments can be steered into the coal-fields to provide productive jobs for ex-miners likely to increase? Issues in energy policy very quickly merge into the broader dilemmas of regional planning and national economic management.

Questions and uncertainties may overhang prospective changes in the energy markets of Britain. Without doubt, however, the next decade will see the fulfilment of many of the promises of the nineteen sixties as the wells and pipelines bring ashore the treasures of the North Sea, as the large new power stations and refineries now under construction come on stream, and as the best examples of highly mechanized mining yield low cost coals. There can be little doubt that, short-term events apart, these highly competitive changes will be accompanied by a continuing abundance of energy for the country's industries and homes.

References

British Association, 'World Fuel and Power Resources', *Advancement of Science* (special issue), September 1965.

Manners, G., *The Geography of Energy*, Hutchinson, 2nd edition, 1971.

Ministry of Power, *The Second Nuclear Power Programme*, Cmnd 2335, 1964.

Ministry of Power, *Fuel Policy*, Cmnd 3438, 1967.

Odell, P. R., *Oil: The New Commanding Height*, Fabian Research Series, No. 251, 1965.

Resources for Britain's Future

Odell, P. R., 'The costs of killing coal', *New Society*, 27 September 1967.

Political and Economic Planning, *A Fuel Policy for Britain*, 1966.

Polanyi, G., *The Price of North Sea Gas*, Hobart Paper No. 38, Institute of Economic Affairs, 1967.

Simpson, E. S., *Coal and the Power Industries in Postwar Britain*, Longman, 1966.

Britain's Overseas Transport Links

by Kenneth Sealy

In the full glare of publicity the first commercial service operated with the Boeing 747 arrived at Heathrow airport on 22 January 1970, thereby inaugurating the much debated era of the big jets. Equally newsworthy are the doings of the Concorde 'twins' on either side of the English Channel and there must be few people who are unaware of the changes in Britain's external communications presaged by these aircraft.

How many people are equally aware of the big changes in the cargo world summed up as 'the container revolution'? The public is more aware of this revolution in transport modes other than shipping and as the Annual Report of the Chamber of Shipping noted, 'shipping the world over, is taken too much for granted'. There are reasons for this; aircraft are predominantly passenger carriers and directly affect us as travellers, while cargo concerns relatively few business people drawn from no single community. The problems and objectives of cargo haulage are complex and, as one shipowner put it, 'surely no industry so homogeneous in its function is so disparate in structure, management and ownership'. External communications by telephone and radio also tend to remain unrecognized except when television links by satellite indicate future potential.

The growth of international passenger travel is one of our more vital developments. The dominance of the aeroplane in this field came in the 1950s, and nowhere more dramatically than on the busy routes over the North Atlantic. Between 1953 and 1963, the percentage of passengers carried by air on the Atlantic routes rose from 36 per cent to 78 per cent, effectively displacing sea travel. On the shorter routes to Europe, except for such specialized service as car ferries, the aeroplane has become a prime carrier, and it is now the major mode of transport in Britain's overseas passenger traffic.

Scheduled traffic on world airlines has been growing at an average annual rate of 14·5 per cent since 1958, while United Kingdom airlines show a growth rate of 15 per cent, very slightly above the world average. Despite the fact that 1968 figures were one per cent down on those for 1967, British airlines still carried 12,200,000 passengers on scheduled services compared with some 4,500,000 carried in ships. In 1969, air traffic recovered from the slack years of 1967 and 1968; British airlines carried 13,200,000 passengers on scheduled services, an increase of 8 per cent over 1968. Still more significant has been the growth in non-scheduled air traffic, the figures for 1968 representing a 16 per cent growth over the previous year and accounting for 3,300,000 passengers, most of whom – 2,700,000 passengers – were carried on charter inclusive tours. Non-scheduled traffic in 1969 was 21 per cent greater than in 1968, accounting for 5,300,000 passengers, of whom 3,700,000 travelled on inclusive tours. The destinations of all these movements to and from Britain emphasize our major ties with Europe and North America.

In 1969 the London airports accounted for 61 per cent of the total passenger traffic, while Heathrow alone handled 50 per cent of the total. The next most important, Manchester Ringway airport, handled only five per cent of the traffic. Contraction in the number of sites handling traffic as it grows in volume and specialization is a feature of many transport systems, but nowhere else in the country is this feature so marked as in air transport. One of the arguments surrounding the proposed third London airport concerns the provision of further capacity in the London area as against elsewhere in the country. Before considering such problems one must look briefly into the future.

The 'jumbo jet' has entered the picture and as more airlines receive these aircraft they will become increasingly familiar additions to airport traffic. By 1972, the journal *Aviation Week* estimates that there will be 143 weekly departures by the Boeing 747 from London, a capacity increase of some 3,000,000 seats a year. When we add the wide-bodied jets for short and medium hauls such as the Lockheed 1011, the DC-10 and the European airbus, the prospect of vastly increased capacity becomes daunting. As far as London is concerned, a new airport will be needed by 1980 or soon after, and it is quite possible that still more airport capacity may be needed to serve the London region before the end of the century. This is quite apart from any capacity that may be generated by vertical take-off and landing (VTOL) developments.

Future expansion throws up enormous problems for the airports, particularly in air traffic control and at the terminals. There are problems to be overcome in terms of both national and international policy as recorded in the Edwards Committee report on British Air Transport in the nineteen seventies. The airlines certainly hope that the promise of larger disposable incomes, increased leisure time and growing business activity will ensure that the customers will demand to be transported, not only to New York in two and a half hours or so at one end of the scale, but on overseas holidays to Europe, the Caribbean, Africa and the Far East. International air travel has still only begun to affect most of the population, for despite the large figures for passengers carried by the airlines, the actual number of United Kingdom residents who travelled on any scheduled service in 1968 was probably not above 3,000,000. Another 2,000,000 may be added for holiday tours, making a total of some 10 per cent of the population.

Cargo transport presents a different face, but one that is hardly less exciting. Once again the major theme is a quickening pace and a growing sophistication beyond our usual picture of 'dirty British coasters'. The ship dominates in both short-sea and deep water routes, while aircraft increasingly nibble at the high value and perishable traffic. As with aircraft on passenger services, cargo transport overseas demands good links with national networks of road and rail.

The size and direction of our foreign trade served by the cargo carriers has shown some quite significant changes since 1945. Trade with Western Europe and the United States has been increasing at the expense of trade with Commonwealth countries, and although bulk cargoes of primary commodities still loom large in sheer volume there has been a growing trade in manufactured goods, in both imports and exports with developed countries in Europe and North America. Our trade with Western Europe is greater than with the Commonwealth and has been since 1962. Bulk commodities, mainly food and raw materials, account for some 70 per cent of the volume, but only 50 per cent of the value of our trade. Trade with the under-developed countries, from which we derived much of our primary produce, has fallen from 25 per cent of total trade in 1953 to 18 per cent in 1967.

Future trade in the various commodity groups has been estimated in studies for the National Ports Council (NPC). As far as imports are concerned, the percentage increase per annum for the period 1965–73 is expected to be less than 5 per cent for food and raw materials, 7 per cent for petroleum imports and increases of 5 to 10 per cent for many manufactured goods. Machinery imports show the highest figure of 11·3 per cent per annum. Rates exceeding 5 per cent for exports include not only manufactured goods but also meat and dairy products, beverages and petroleum products. The least known feature here is probably the importance of manufactured goods in our import trade.

Unlike passenger traffic where the 'commodity' is fairly homo-geneous, cargo presents a bewildering array of weights, shapes and sizes. Specialization in cargo transport may be expected to show more than one type of development to cope with such varied require-ments. As far as general merchandise trade is concerned, most is carried in cargo liners and tramps, with London and Liverpool as the main ports. In terms of sheer tonnage handled these two ports are outclassed by some of the specialized bulk handling ports such as Milford Haven or the Medway ports importing crude oil.

The evolution of bulk carriage is best known through the steep rise in the size of oil tankers since 1950 and the development of harbours to handle them, but the principle also applies to other cargoes that can be carried in bulk such as other liquids, grain, ores or sugar. Not so obvious from general figures of tonnage handled is the increasing importance of a whole group of distribution chains coping with palletized and containerized traffic designed to give a less interrupted flow from factory to customer. Here the big ports like London and Liverpool play a part, but new installations in smaller ports like Preston, Harwich and Felixstowe have risen in importance.

Without underestimating the importance of general cargo ports, it is reasonable to concentrate on the major developments in bulk handling and container methods. Economies of scale apply to the operation of ships as to other industrial processes and where the traffic is great enough and amenable to bulk handling, there has been pressure to take advantage of the lower operating costs of bigger vessels. Optimum ship size also varies with the speed of handling; a case of matching ship and port. Since some 75 per cent of our sea-borne cargo is accounted for by bulk commodities, there is a strong case for specialization.

The establishment of oil refineries on British and European coasts since 1945 has increased the volume of crude oil imports as opposed to the pre-war imports of semi-refined and refined products from overseas refineries sited on the oilfields. With this change to a more homogeneous import product, the possibility of using very large tankers became feasible. In 1951 the largest tankers in world fleets reached 32,000 tons dead-weight, by 1963 the figure reached 132,000 tons and currently figures up to 500,000 tons are being considered. Such ships cannot be handled in shallow estuaries, and the deep water terminals at Milford Haven, on the Clyde and the Whiddy Island terminal at Bantry Bay in Eire are examples of both existing and proposed sites. Subsequent distribution may be by pipeline or by smaller tankers, the latter also playing a part in the increasing short-sea traffic in refined products.

Bulk handling of other cargoes has followed. Iron ore is the country's largest single dry cargo import, 16,000,000 tons being imported in 1967, while the NPC estimates for 1973 give a figure of 24,000,000 tons. The lower costs of foreign ores and their higher iron content favour this trend and ore imports are another candidate for bulk handling. Even if most of the imported ore were to be palletized, the NPC expects that this would reduce the tonnage figures by less than 10 per cent. It has been estimated that the freight saving from using an 85,000 ton dead-weight carrier as against one of 20,000 tons dead-weight on a deep sea route would be 75 p per ton of ore, and this figure might be still more in the long run. Ore carriers of up to 100,000 tons dead-weight are in use, and increased use of these large vessels may be expected in the future. The main British port designed to handle such vessels is the tidal harbour at Port Talbot serving the Margam steel-works. In this case the main market for the ore is adjacent to the port, but development of other bulk port installations such as the Tilbury Grain Terminal or the Immingham coal terminal, demands adequate connections with internal transport. In the long term, new processing facilities for such bulk cargoes may be expected to be located near the terminals, reducing the need for long inland hauls. The development of facilities to receive grain from the Tilbury terminal is taking place adjacent to the terminal site, but inland distribution will still be necessary for a considerable proportion of the tonnage.

General cargo accounts for some 25 per cent of the volume of our overseas trade, but in value it accounts for at least half of the total. Most of this cargo travels in tramp vessels or cargo liners from many ports. Increased trade with Europe has stressed the importance of the short-sea routes and encouraged improved distribution, while increases in deep water trade, especially with the United States, have also made demands on our shipping. This is not only because of increased traffic, but also because of competition from overseas fleets.

General cargo comes in all sorts of shapes, sizes and values and the problems of rationalizing such traffic in terms of bulk carriage are considerable. Much time is spent in dealing with numbers of small consignments, particularly in consolidating shipments and handling them at the ports. It is hardly surprising that up to 60 per cent of a cargo liner's time may be spent in port; and that only 15 per cent of port time is spent in actually loading or unloading. It has been suggested that a decrease of 20 per cent in port time would reduce the cost of sea transport by between 18 and 35 per cent depending on the route. It is against this background that we should look at the development of pallet and container systems. Their advantages in improving distribution have been known for some time. In 1964 it was estimated that palletizing cargo could reduce the turnround at ports by up to 50 per cent and reduce stevedoring costs.

The principle behind all the systems of pallet or container operations is that distribution from factory to customer should be considered as a single flow with minimum interruption. The distinction between land and sea and the need to trans-ship from one vehicle to another at the coastline represents the chief break in the chain. To

10. *To allow bulk handling of iron ore, ships are designed with large, uninterrupted holds. These are accessible to overhead gantry cranes which enable rapid discharge. A cargo of 27,000 tons of ore is unloaded at South Bank Wharf which adjoins the British Steel Corporation's Cleveland Works.*

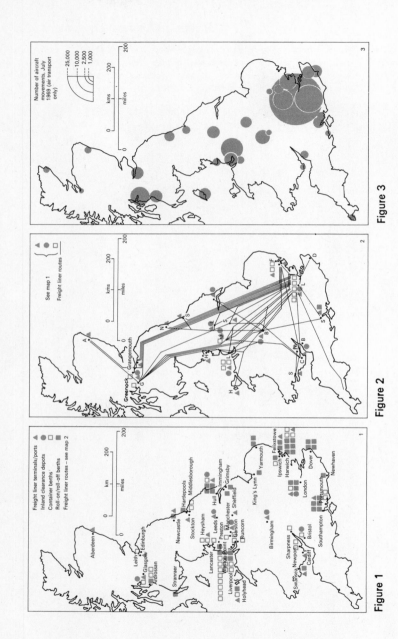

Figure 1

Freight liner terminals/ports ▲
Inland clearance depots ●
Container berths ☐
Roll-on/roll-off berths ◼
Freight liner routes – see map 2

0   miles   200
0   km   200

Aberdeen
Leith
Edinburgh
Glasgow
Ardrossan
Stranraer
Newcastle
Hartlepools
Stockton
Middlesborough
Heysham
Lancaster
Preston
Leeds
Hull
Birmingham
Grimsby
Manchester
Sheffield
Liverpool
Weston Point
Garston
Runcorn
Holyhead
King's Lynn
Yarmouth
Birmingham
Ipswich
Felixstowe
Harwich
Sharpness
Newport
London
Cardiff
Swansea
Bristol
Portsmouth
Southampton
Dover
Newhaven

Figure 2

See map 1   ▲ ● ☐
Freight liner routes

0   miles   200
0   kms   200

A
Greenock
G
Grangemouth
F
L
D
S
N
B
C
H

Figure 3

Number of aircraft movements, July 1969 (air transport only)

25,000
10,000
2,500
1,000

0   kms   200
0   miles   200

get over this potential bottleneck one can either roll the land unit on to the ship or handle the cargo in large homogeneous units that can be quickly transferred. Combinations of these possibilities form the foundation of all the various pallet and container systems, adjusted to the needs of either short-sea or deep water routes. The less expensive pallet is a simpler version of the container, more easily stored when not in use, more flexible and less expensive than the container, which costs from £500 to £800 per unit. The advantage of the container is that, once packed, it is handled throughout its journey as a single unit.

The individual methods that make use of this 'through delivery' service vary according to the route chosen. For the important short-sea routes to Europe or Ireland the roll-on/roll-off system is an example. Here the container moves from the factory or warehouse to the port on a trailer. The tractor is unhitched and trailer and container are loaded as a unit on to the ship. Alternatively the container may be transported by truck or train to the quay and loaded by fork lift, again reducing the handling procedure.

Deep sea traffic can be handled by lifting the container from truck or train into specially designed vessels in much the same way. The ship itself has a cellular type of hold enabling containers to be rapidly loaded with a minimum of delay. Given the volume of traffic, these methods have drastically reduced the total travel time for consignments and increased the working capacity of the ships. The busy North Atlantic routes have so far become the most advanced container routes, but the practice is spreading to Far Eastern and Australian routes.

The use of containers in international trade demands agreement with respect to the size, strength and handling procedures between countries. Discussions between fifteen countries and three international bodies produced the first generally accepted definition of a container recorded by the International Standards Organization in 1968.

Apart from technical considerations of container and container-ship geometry, there is the wider issue of how much of our trade is suitable for container transport and how much may be more economically carried in conventional cargo vessels using improved facilities to cut handling time. Suitable cargoes are drawn primarily from manufactured goods and, to a lesser extent, from goods in the food and drink categories.

Allocation to routes and ports depends on the distinction between short-sea and deep water trades. Short-sea routes to Europe are likely to increase rapidly in importance, but there will be competition from 'all-land' routes to destinations such as the Mediterranean cities and the possible diversion through the proposed Channel Tunnel. Up to the present, the effect of the latter is difficult to judge, but some substitution is almost certain. Deep water expansion will come, not only from the North Atlantic traffic, but increasingly on routes to India, the Far East and Australasia.

Air cargo's place in our external trade has shown a growth rate of 13·4 per cent per annum over the last decade, mainly in the transport of high value or perishable goods. These include physically perishable goods and those where time is at a premium. In terms of value Heathrow ranks as Britain's third port, whereas in terms of volume it is relatively insignificant. The use of standard containers in the new jets combined with the much greater capacity represented by these aircraft will make airlines increasingly alert to cargo traffic.

To try to sum up these varied aspects of our external communications is a daunting task. Concentration on only part of the whole leaves out such elements as the transmission of information, a vital part of our total system. Demand for telephone and radio links has been stimulated as trade has grown and there are future possibilities of extending transmitted, rather than transported, data. Just to what extent developments in transmitted computer data or the use of facsimile transmission will reduce the need for business travel, or increase it, is an intriguing question. The possibilities of VTOL aircraft, hovercraft or the Channel Tunnel have not been fully realized and their roles will be much clearer by the end of the decade than they are at present. A common problem area concerns terminals in air, land and sea transport, since increasing specialization and volume of trade focuses forcibly on these points of interchange.

References

British Airports Authority, *Report and Accounts* (Annual), HMSO.

Goss, R. O., *Studies in Maritime Economics*, CUP, 1968.

National Economic Development Office, *Through Transport to Europe*, HMSO, 1966.

National Ports Council
  Digest of Port Statistics, (Annual).
  Cargo Management in the Seventies, 1968.
  Containerisation on the North Atlantic; a port-to-port analysis and the 1970 outlook for deep sea container service, Arthur D. Little, 1967.
  Port Progress Report, 1969.

Report of the Committee of Inquiry into Civil Air Transport (Edwards Report), *British Air Transport in the Seventies*, Cmnd 4018, HMSO, 1969.

Sealy, K. R., 'Integration of Air and Surface Transport', in *World Airports – The Way Ahead*, Institution of Civil Engineers, 1970.

Van den Burg, G., *Containerisation: a modern transport system*, Hutchinson, 1969.

Some Consequences of Change

Water Resources

by Judith Rees

Recognition of the need for water resource planning on a national scale has only come in comparatively recent years. Traditionally, consumers of water had been left to develop their resources independently on a local basis. No restrictions were placed on water abstractions, and anyone wishing to obtain a water supply merely acquired land alongside a water-course or above water-bearing strata. Little, if any, integration occurred within the supply system; it was common for water supply plants to be constructed for specific purposes with little consideration of the potential capacity of the sites. Indeed, while demands were relatively small, and capable of being satisfied by piecemeal local and specific developments, it could safely be argued that if the parts were right there was no need to worry about the whole. However, during the late 1930s overpumping of some ground water sources and general water shortages led to the view that some form of central control was necessary to avoid the haphazard and wasteful exploitation of our water resources.

The beginnings of a modern water conservation and development policy can be seen in the 1945 Water Act, which put upon the 'Minister' (now the Secretary of State for the Environment) the duty 'to promote the conservation and proper use of water resources and the provision of water supplies in England and Wales, and to secure the effective execution by water undertakings under his control and direction, of a national policy relating to water'. For the first time abstractors taking ground water in overexploited areas were required to obtain licences for any new or additional abstraction. In an attempt to rationalize and increase the economic viability of water undertakings, the Government has pressed for a large reduction in the number of local supply authorities. This pressure has resulted in a marked decline in the number of undertakings from over 1,100 immediately after the war to 192 today. Local competition for resources has therefore been reduced as the extended undertakings are able to integrate supplies over wider areas. As far as the development of water resources for the future is concerned, perhaps the most fundamental improvement in the administration of the water industry has been the establishment of comprehensive regional control over all users in England and Wales. This measure was introduced by the 1963 Water Resources Act. River authorities were established with responsibility for the co-ordination of all water uses in river basins, and the Water Resources Board was set up with the duty to promote the national integration of resource development.

The main factor which has stimulated these administrative changes has been the increased demand for water from all sectors of the economy. Local sources could no longer cope satisfactorily with the situation and a broader view became essential. In the same way the present concern with the purity of our rivers and their use for recreation may well promote further administrative changes in the near future. There is already some doubt whether the responsibility for disposing of sewage can be left in local authority hands, especially when the river authorities are reluctant to prosecute authorities which are neglecting their responsibilities.

Water undertakings, which comprise the public supply industry, are responsible for abstracting water from surface and underground sources and distributing it to households, shops, farms and factories. Since 1945 these undertakings have experienced demand increases of between 2 and 3·5 per cent per annum. Consistently increases in water demands have outpaced the rate of population increase; a trend which reflects, amongst other things, improved housing standards, improved standards of factory hygiene, increased ownership of water-using consumer goods, and also the extension of piped water facilities into rural areas. Water engineers have forecast that demand will continue to increase by approximately 3 per cent per annum, which implies that, by the year 2000, undertakings will be supplying an average of at least 360 litres per day to every person living in Britain. This figure will probably be made up of about 250 litres used in houses and shops and the remainder used in factories. Since 1961, however, there has been a marked slackening

11. *Clywedog dam on the River Severn is designed to regulate the flow of water to provide for future increases in water abstraction by Birmingham Corporation. The use of existing streams to transport the commodity to demand centres reduces costs of supply and encourages re-use of the water between the regulatory reservoir and the distant urban centre.*

off in the rate of increase in demand for water from undertakings, which may mean that 360 litres per head daily will not be required until well into the twenty-first century. Although the actual rate of increase is open to question there is no doubt that undertakings will have to cope with an expansion of demand due both to population changes and an increasing per capita consumption, unless the present pricing methods are altered.

Most undertakings use two different methods of charging consumers for their water supply. On the one hand, industrial and agricultural concerns are given a metered supply and they pay for each unit of 4,550 litres used. On the other hand, no record is kept of the amount of water taken by domestic and most commercial consumers; they pay a fixed charge, the water rate, and are entitled to use as much water as they want. As extra litres of water can be obtained without cost the householder has no incentive to economize and avoid waste. It has been suggested that if domestic consumers were metered and charged for each litre of water taken, there would be an absolute decrease in the amount of water used, and possibly a permanently lower rate of increase in demand in the future. Certainly metering should reduce the wasteful use of the resource. A complete change in the charging system by introducing meters into every property is unlikely to take place in the very near future as the costs would be prohibitive. There is, however, an increasing number of progressive water engineers who foresee metering as a possibility by the 1980s, at least for new properties. If this is indeed the case, demand forecasts and capacity extension schemes will have to be reconsidered.

In addition to the water abstracted by water undertakings, a considerably larger quantity is taken *privately* by farmers and by industry. In relative terms agricultural demands for private abstraction water are small, accounting for some 1,136 million litres per day out of the 109,000 million litres per day abstracted in total. However, this agricultural use is significant because the bulk of it is taken for irrigation during the peak demand and low flow period, and because virtually all of it passes into the atmosphere, with no return for re-use.

Irrigation has been practised in this country for many years to increase the yield of high value market garden crops. Since the 1950s, however, irrigation of grass, cereals and potatoes has become relatively common practice and this has much greater implications for water resource development. By 1961 enough irrigation equipment existed to water over 53,000 hectares of crops and this increased by an average of 6,000 hectares per annum until 1967. Technically over 600,000 hectares of crops in England and Wales could benefit from irrigation but it is unlikely that such a maximum will ever be achieved. Future expansion of the irrigated acreage is likely to be slower than in past years, since farmers are now required to pay for each 4,550 litres that they are licensed to abstract. Prices for water used in irrigation vary between different parts of the country, but are always relatively high at over 1·7 p per 4,550 litres, since little, if any, water is returned for re-use. The highest charges for irrigation water are imposed by the Essex River Authority. In this area irrigators using water from an inland source during the summer months are charged 6 p per 4,550 litres. Doubts on the economic viability of irrigating many crops were cast by Nix (1968) even before pricing of water occurred and it is now highly probable that grass, cereals and sugar beet irrigation will decline in importance. Irrigation of potatoes and market-garden crops will continue, however, as yield increases are high enough to allow a good net return even if water costs as much as 20 p per 4,550 litres. In addition to the increased amount of water used for irrigation, farmers have also demanded greater quantities to improve standards of cleanliness in dairies, and to spray crops as protection from frost and insect pests. The amount of water involved in these uses is relatively minor, and future increases should not impose strain on developed resources.

At the present time approximately 109,000 million litres are abstracted each day from surface and ground water sources in England and Wales. As much as 80 per cent of this is taken privately, directly from source, by manufacturers, and in addition industry also buys one third of all water abstracted by undertakings, 20,500 million litres. Clearly, industry is by far the greatest water user, especially as considerable use is also made of water still in streams for effluent disposal. It must, however, be pointed out that a very high proportion of industrial abstraction occurs to provide cooling water, which is returned to source with little diminution in quality or quantity. In fact approximately 68,000 litres per day are taken by the Central Electricity Generating Board alone for cooling at power stations.

If present trends continue the amount of water abstracted will have doubled by the end of the century. However, it appears that industrialists are planning to decrease their gross consumption. Gross usage is the actual amount withdrawn from a water source, whereas net use is gross usage minus the quantity of water returned to the water source. The new charges, which came into effect on 1 April 1969, and the increasing difficulty of extending private abstraction, are encouraging firms to install recycling equipment, and even to alter their processes in order to reduce gross water usage. In fact it has already been suggested that as prices increase firms will want to reduce the quantity of water that they are licensed to abstract when the licences come up for renewal. As firms pay for each unit of 4,550 litres which they are licensed to take, they will want to reduce the amount on the licence if the actual consumption falls short of this. The consumption of water purchased from local undertakings may well also increase less rapidly in the future since many firms are responding to the increasing meter charges by re-using their supplies.

Undoubtedly in the future large users of cooling water will have to locate more and more to estuarine and coastal sites: a trend which is already well established. The location of other industry, however, is unlikely to be greatly affected by the availability of water supplies, at least in the foreseeable future. River authorities are highly unlikely absolutely to prohibit all extensions of industrial abstractions; at worst, industry will be faced with higher water prices and curtailing of the rate of increase in water use. In this case it will usually be far more economic for firms to accept the price rise and install re-using equipment rather than to consider an alternative location. Water costs are normally a minor element in the cost structure of firms; variations in the cost or availability of land, labour and raw materials are much more important influences on industrial location.

In addition to increases in extractive uses of water there has been, and will continue to be, a rapid expansion in the demand for water used *in situ*. Much of the increased use of water actually within the stream courses can be attributed to recreation demands. The other *in situ* uses, which include power generation, commercial navigation, and dilution of effluent and sewage, are highly unlikely to increase in the future. Commercial navigation on inland waterways has declined markedly since World War II, and this decline is expected to continue as water transport faces keen competition from road, rail, and pipeline. It is important to note that virtually as much water and capital are required to maintain navigable ways whether one or many boats use the facilities. Therefore, in view of the declining traffic the unit costs of using water for commercial navigation are increasing sharply.

Dilution of effluent and sewage in rivers has been strictly controlled since the 1951 and 1961 Rivers Acts, resulting in a noticeable reduction in the level of pollution in recent years in some rivers, for example the Thames. Effluent discharges now have to be authorized by the river authorities and, if discharge is allowed, limits are usually imposed on the quantity, temperature, and composition of the effluent. Similarly, there are now stricter controls on the amount and type of effluent discharged by firms into local authority sewers. Both industry and local sewage authorities have increased their capital investment in purification equipment. For example, it has been estimated that the firms now within the British Steel Corporation spent over £4·5 million on improving the quality of their effluent between 1960 and 1966. In view of public pressure to improve river quality, it is certain that industry and local authorities will increasingly have to accept the costs imposed by their waste disposal, rather than being able to transfer some of these costs to other water users. If carried far enough the drive to reduce river pollution could result in large increases in conventional water supplies. For example, a substantial reduction in the effluent and sewage discharge from the Birmingham conurbation could well result in the Trent being used as a source of water for the East Midland area.

As has already been mentioned, the greatest future demands for water will come from recreation interests. Dramatic increases in such water-based activities as yachting, fishing, and water skiing have already taken place; with increased leisure time and greater affluence future increases must be expected. It is no longer doubted that recreation is a legitimate use of water. The 1963 Water Resources Act, for example, has empowered river authorities to make provision for recreation, and the Government white paper *Leisure in the Countryside* (1966) has stressed that reservoirs could and should be available for recreation use.

There is great scope for extending the multiple use of reservoirs as water engineers become less cautious about maintaining the high purity standards of their supplies. It should, of course, be realized that all recreation use of water imposes costs; for example, a local authority may have to install additional purification equipment, as well as provide such facilities as access roads, car parks, toilets, slipways, and fish hatcheries. There would appear to be no logical objection to asking the public to pay for these additional facilities and it should become more common in the future for people to pay for their recreational use of water.

Having discussed the likely future increases in the demand for water, it remains to see whether these demands can be satisfied, and if so by what methods. Although it is fairly common to hear that parts of England have water shortage problems, this does not imply that there are physical difficulties in extending supplies. With a renewable and re-usable resource like water there is always more available at a price, and in the last resort the sea represents a virtually inexhaustible supply. Our shortages are purely economic, with the amount of water demanded at the going price being greater than that supplied. Many of the present shortages are accentuated by the fact that many users of water do not pay the full cost of their supply. Today this is still true of domestic users as well as those that make use of recreation, effluent and sewage disposal facilities. But until recently the situation was much worse as 'free' water was available to all abstractors before the licence charges were introduced. In such a situation it was hardly surprising that water authorities found themselves in financial difficulties when they attempted to satisfy all competing demands. In the future it is highly likely that more and more water users will be asked to pay the full costs involved in providing their supply. This should have the effect both of reducing demand increases and of giving the authorities more revenue to increase supplies.

Economic shortages, where the provision of capacity falls behind demand, could occur in most parts of Britain. They are by no means confined to south-east England, where low rainfall and high evapo-transpiration rates, coupled with a high density of water users, exacerbate the situation. Economic shortages have occurred in the Manchester area and in Western Scotland despite the relatively high rainfall.

Throughout England and Wales it is likely that supply can most economically be equated with demand by developing new conventional sources of water, at least until the late 1970s. These conventional sources, which will include new pumpings from aquifers and the provision of additional storage reservoirs, will be linked to demand centres by pipeline, or more commonly by existing river channels. Supplies may also be increased by encouraging the successive re-use of water, purification of sewage and effluent, and by recharging aquifers artificially. Without doubt most new schemes

12. *As it becomes increasingly difficult to obtain water from conventional sources, more attention is being paid to the economic feasibility of supplying water from desalination plants. An electrodialysis plant at Manningtree, Essex, is successfully producing over 225,000 litres of fresh water each day from brackish ground water. Operational costs increase with the salinity of feed water, so that this method cannot yet be used economically to produce fresh water from the sea.*

will involve much greater capital expenditure than previous developments, since the easiest and nearest sources have long been exploited.

A major feature of many of the future schemes will be their regional character with much greater cooperation between river authorities. The regional nature of schemes will be inevitable given the increased distance that water will have to be transported before use. This is not to imply that anything like a water grid will be constructed in Britain, although various schemes for a national grid have been put forward. One such suggestion is that a Grand Contour Canal should be established, which would run from Newcastle to Manchester and then south to Bristol, Southampton and London. The canal would be used for navigation and private abstraction as well as providing the south-east with water from the north and west. This scheme, like the other grid proposals, is prohibitively expensive at the present time, and is unlikely ever to be the cheapest means of providing water. Any long distance transport of a bulky, low value commodity like water is rarely economically feasible, unless movement with gravity and without pumping can take place.

Conventional schemes may still be able to provide for increased water demands in most areas after 1980, although it is possible that the increasing cost of water from these sources will make barrage schemes and desalination economically feasible by this date. Various barrage schemes have been proposed, the most important being those located at the Wash, Dee, Solway and Morecambe Bay (Figure 1). At the moment it does not look as if the Wash scheme will be able to compete with conventional water sources until after the year 2000. From the Water Resources Board's report on water supplies for south-east England, it appears that the capital expenditure involved in providing water conventionally would be approximately £90 million less than the cost of the Wash barrage (Figure 2). If these estimates prove correct it must be very doubtful whether the Wash scheme will ever be developed, since by 2000 it is highly likely that desalination will be economic. This is not to suggest that no barrage schemes will be constructed at all. On present information it appears that either the Solway or Morecambe Bay barrages could be economic methods of providing water for the north-west and north-east. Although water from these schemes may still be more expensive than from some conventional sources, the schemes could well be acceptable given the political difficulties encountered in developing surface reservoirs. The Dee scheme may also prove to be economic when the benefits of providing a road link across the estuary are added to those of increasing the region's water supplies.

Perhaps the greatest difficulty in forecasting the likely sources of future water supplies lies in attempting to predict the likely changes in the cost of desalted water. It appears to be assumed by the water industry that barrages will be developed before desalination becomes economic, but there are dangers in this assumption. If barrages are developed ahead of demand there is a distinct possibility that decreasing desalination costs could cause barrages to be left as rather expensive white elephants used primarily for recreation. Given

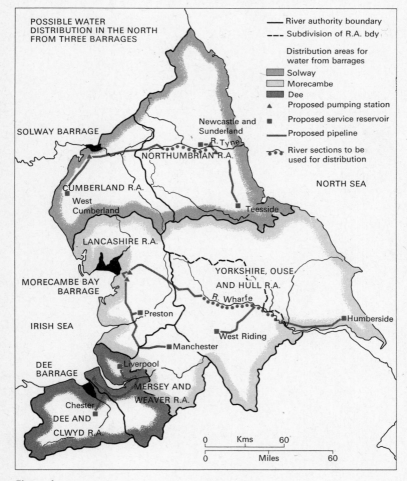

Figure 1

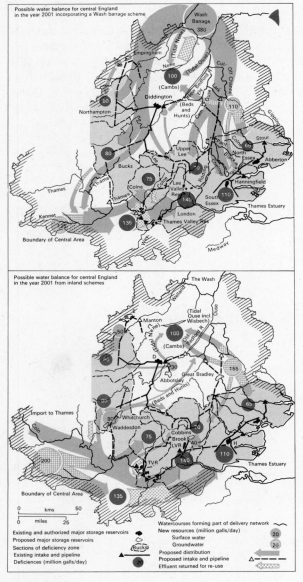

Figure 2

the uncertainties in forecasting cost changes, there is a strong case for developing a barrage's capacity in stages. If the present trend of declining desalting costs continues, it appears feasible to suggest that desalination could make a significant contribution to our water supplies by the late 1980s or 1990s. Certainly in a county like Essex relatively small decreases in the cost of desalination would ensure its serious consideration. Conventional schemes producing water at over 25 p per 4,550 litres are already envisaged in this county and at the present time dual purpose distillation plants can produce water at from 21 p to 28 p. Distillation plants are likely to be first used in conjunction with a conventional reservoir, to provide water only at low flow and peak demand periods. These distillation plants will be incorporated in dual purpose schemes linked to a nuclear power station. During the winter electricity generation will be the sole function of the station, but during the off-peak period for electricity demand, power could be made available for distillation. Such schemes are particularly attractive since peak demands for water coincide with off-peak demands for electricity, and so nuclear power stations could be utilized to capacity all year round.

In the future capital expenditure on providing water will increase rapidly, and as it does so water supply should continue to lose its social service character, and become more like an industry. One element in this change will probably be the trend towards pricing water like any other commodity. Abstraction charges have already been introduced, and some charges for pollution and recreational uses of water will probably come in the future. There is also the possibility that householders will be asked to pay for the actual water they take rather than be given a water service after payment of a flat rate. Another feature in the changing nature of water provision will be the possibly more restricted role of the engineer, resulting from the transference of his investment decision-making and management roles to the accountant and economist. Certainly when desalination becomes the basic method of providing additional water a whole new era in water supply will begin. While the collection and distribution of 'natural' water will still be an important function of the water industry, it will become somewhat like the electricity and gas industries, being a monopolistic producer of a manufactured good.

References

Bird, P. A., and Jackson, C. I., 'Economic Charges for Water' in *Essays in the Theory and Practice of Pricing*. Readings in Political Economy, 3, London, Institute of Economic Affairs, 1967.

Burley, M. J., and Mawer, P. A., 'The Present State of Desalination', *Water and Water Engineering*, Vol. 72, pp. 368–70, 1968.

Essex River Authority, *Charging Scheme*, 1968, revised 1970.

Institution of Civil Engineers, *Conservation of Water Resources in the United Kingdom*, Proceedings of a Symposium, October 1962, London, 1963.

Kavanagh, N. J., 'The Economics of the Recreational Use of Rivers and Reservoirs', *Water and Water Engineering*, Vol. 72, pp. 401–8, 1968.

Nix, J. S., 'The Economics of Farm Crop Irrigation in Great Britain', *Journal of the Chartered Land Agent's Society*, Vol. 67, pp. 196–201, 1968.

Rees, J. A., *Industrial Demand for Water. A study of South-East England*, Weidenfeld & Nicolson, 1969.

Rees, J. A., and Rees, R., *Demand Forecasts and Capacity Margins in South-East England* (typescript).

Rowntree, N. A. F., and Ineson, J., *Symposium on the Conservation and Use of Water Resources in the United Kingdom*, British Association, September 1966.

Town and Country Planning Association, *Town and Country Planning*, Special issue on 'Water and Planning', June 1966.

United Kingdom Government, *Water Act, 1945*, HMSO, 1945.

United Kingdom Government, *Rivers Act, 1951*, HMSO, 1951.

United Kingdom Government, *Rivers Act, 1961*, HMSO, 1961.

United Kingdom Government, *Water Resources Act, 1963*, HMSO, 1963.

United Kingdom Government, *Water Conservation in England and Wales*, Cmnd 1693, HMSO, 1962.

United Kingdom Government, *Leisure in the Countryside, England and Wales*, Cmnd 2928, HMSO, 1966.

United Kingdom Government, Office of the Minister of Science, *Irrigation in Great Britain*, HMSO, 1962.

United Kingdom Government, Water Resources Board, Report No. 1, *Water Supplies in South East England*, HMSO, 1966.

United Kingdom Government, Water Resources Board, Report No. 4, *Morecambe Bay and Solway Barrages*, Report on Desk Studies, HMSO, 1967.

United Kingdom Government, Water Resources Board, Report No. 6, *Desalination for England and Wales*, HMSO, 1969.

United Kingdom Government, Water Resources Board, 1967–8, *Fifth Annual Report*, HMSO, 1968.

New Regions for Old*

by Peter Haggett

Local and regional government provide the essential links in the chain connecting central government with local communities. The efficiency of that chain is likely to be judged in different ways. To a Whitehall department the number of regions must be small enough to allow each unit to meet certain minimum thresholds of efficient management; to a local community the number of regions must be large enough to allow a local voice on local problems. One deciding factor in the argument is that local government is extremely costly and that the numbers involved in servicing this 'chain of command' is on the increase.

It is of course to be expected that as Britain, in common with the other West European countries, moves into its 'post industrial' phase, so the proportion of workers in the information and control sectors should increase. What is perhaps less palatable is that with growth comes the probability that the criteria of efficiency originally applied to industrial organizations will be also applied to service industries. The first signs of mergers, rationalizations, shake-outs and the like are already apparent in office industries as unlike as the BBC and Pools promotions.

For English local government the most dramatic foretaste of rationalization has come in the publication of the Royal Commission Report on Local Government – the Redcliffe-Maud report – in June 1969. With a change in government in the summer of 1970 the final

* Since this chapter went to press, the Conservative government have published white papers outlining their proposals for local government reform. As expected, they are less radical than those of the Redcliffe–Maud report. The total number of authorities in England (outside Greater London) is to be reduced to 44, based largely on the existing counties. Six of the units are designated as Metropolitan Counties and are further subdivided into districts. Proposals for the pattern of districts within the non-metropolitan counties are still to be evolved.

action that will be taken on the Royal Commission's report is still not clear. At the time of writing, the indications are that the Conservative government is likely to favour a less radical restructuring than that recommended in the report; for example, the traditional county units may continue to play an important role. Whatever government is in office however, the basic issues of spatial reorganization remain similar to those faced by the service industries.

Unlike the reorganization of the private sector in which the critical evidence of change is limited to restricted research reports and boardroom minutes, this projected shake-up of local and regional government has been accompanied by massive publicity and intense public debate. Its proposals are therefore already well known, at least in broad terms. England, outside London, would be divided into sixty-one new local government areas (Figure 1). In fifty-eight of these new areas one authority (the unitary authority) would become responsible for all local government services but in the remaining areas (Merseyside; Selnec, which consists of south-east Lancashire and north-east and central Cheshire; and the West Midlands) services would be divided between two tiers of authority. In the three metropolitan area authorities, key functions would be planning, transportation, major development and housing policy. In the lower-tier authorities, the metropolitan districts (four in Merseyside, nine in Selnec and seven in the West Midlands) would control education, the personal social services, house building and house management. The sixty-one areas, together with Greater London, would be grouped into eight provinces, each with its own representative provincial council. Councils would be elected indirectly by the main authorities and would 'settle the broad economic, land use and investment framework for the planning and development of unitary and metropolitan authorities'.

What would happen to the existing framework of local and regional government under the Redcliffe–Maud proposals? At the upper end of the spectrum the provincial councils would replace the present regional economic planning councils. In the unitary areas, local councils would continue to be elected for the area of each present county borough, borough and urban district but the functions of these councils would be curtailed. In the metropolitan areas there would

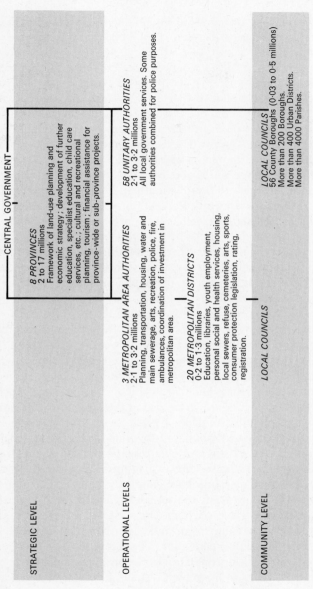

STRATEGIC LEVEL

CENTRAL GOVERNMENT

8 PROVINCES
2 to 17 millions
Framework of land-use planning and economic strategy; development of further education, specialist education, child care services, etc.; cultural and recreational planning, tourism; financial assistance for province-wide or sub-province projects.

58 UNITARY AUTHORITIES
2·1 to 3·2 millions
All local government services. Some authorities combined for police purposes.

OPERATIONAL LEVELS

3 METROPOLITAN AREA AUTHORITIES
2·1 to 3·2 millions
Planning, transportation, housing, water and main sewerage, arts, recreation, police, fire, ambulances, coordination of investment in metropolitan area.

20 METROPOLITAN DISTRICTS
0·2 to 1·3 millions
Education, libraries, youth employment, personal social and health services, housing, local sewers, refuse, cemeteries, arts, sports, consumer protection legislation, rating, registration.

LOCAL COUNCILS

COMMUNITY LEVEL

LOCAL COUNCILS
56 County Boroughs (0·03 to 0·5 millions)
More than 200 Boroughs.
More than 400 Urban Districts.
More than 4000 Parishes.

Figure 1   Pattern of functions within the government structure proposed by the Redcliffe-Maud report.

be local councils wherever the inhabitants want one. Parish councils would continue to be elected wherever there is now a parish council.

Some idea of the contrast between the existing and the proposed structures is shown in the set of maps on south-west England (Figure 2). The six counties and six county boroughs that make up the present South West Economic Planning Region would be replaced by an enlarged South Western Province made up of eight unitary authorities. The province with a population of 4,060,000 and an area over 24,000 square kilometres shows small increases of 7 per cent in population and 3 per cent in area over the existing region. The major additions to the unit are Bournemouth and adjoining parts of Hampshire (replacing the arbitrary Poole–Bournemouth boundary) plus a small part of Berkshire which has economic links with Swindon. The twelve existing county units have a greater variation in size and resources than the new units that replaced them. For the country as a whole the new units show a reduction in the present coefficient of variability of about 23 per cent for population, 56 per cent for area, and 16 per cent for total rateable value; in other words, the new units are considerably more homogeneous than those they replace.

In a substantial minority report, Derek Senior proposed a second, fundamentally altered structure based on a two-tier system of thirty-five upper level and 148 lower level city regions. Senior's South Western Province departs in gross structure and internal divisions both from the existing boundaries and from the Redcliffe–Maud proposals. The inclusion of Hereford in the North-west Region and the exclusion of most of Dorset gives an elongated region in the South-west including a population split into four main city regions – Plymouth, Exeter, Bristol and Gloucester – and thirteen districts.

Despite their differences the two reports have certain common features. The final map in Figure 2 indicates some common areas of overlap in the South-west: the somewhat isolated 'rump shires' of Cornwall, Devon, Somerset, Wiltshire and Gloucester, each centering on their existing county town, and the urban field centres of Plymouth, Bristol and Bournemouth. In both reports all the counties are much reduced in size, while Dorset disappears completely in a proposed merger with Bournemouth. About 40 per cent of the area is made up by three disputed areas: east Cornwall and north Devon, Torbay, and a strip running from mid-Somerset through north Wiltshire to east Gloucestershire. In these areas there is little common

Figure 2

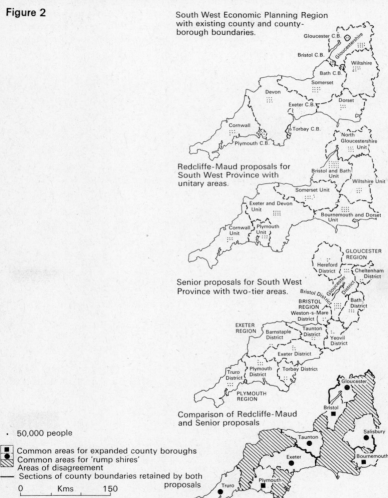

South West Economic Planning Region with existing county and county-borough boundaries.

Redcliffe-Maud proposals for South West Province with unitary areas.

Senior proposals for South West Province with two-tier areas.

Comparison of Redcliffe-Maud and Senior proposals

- 50,000 people

■ Common areas for expanded county boroughs
● Common areas for 'rump shires'
▨ Areas of disagreement
— Sections of county boundaries retained by both proposals

0 —— Kms —— 150
0 —— Miles —— 150

13. *The city of Bath shows most of the problems facing the Royal Commission on Local Government. Existing boundaries fail to incorporate major housing developments built in response to demands generated by expansion in employment in the city; these areas fall within parishes administered by Somerset County from Taunton. Bath is also tied by employment and service links to Bristol and a proposal to join the two into a common Bath–Bristol unit forms one of the more controversial proposals of the Royal Commission. Local opinion shows a strong preference for the* status quo.

ground between the two reports and it is precisely here that debate over boundaries is likely to be at its strongest.

The basis on which the new units proposed in the Redcliffe–Maud report were planned is clearly spelt out. The first criteria used were the characteristics of 'coherence' and 'self-containment'. In practice this meant using the evidence of the 1966 census on journey-to-work movements, supplemented by analyses of public transport services and newspaper circulation. Organizational structure, which includes the spatial structure of professional, government and business organizations, was also considered. Despite the difficulties of defining watertight catchment areas it is argued that the new town–country units will be more effective for land use and transportation planning and for local government as a whole.

The attempt to bring unit boundaries into line with the contemporary 'socio-geographic facts of British life' has led to a series of compromises around which some vigorous debates are emerging. In the South-west, the proposals for the Bristol–Bath area are particularly contentious. Under the new Redcliffe-Maud proposals this would become a single unit with an area of 2,200 square kilometres, and a population of 1,010,000. The argument for combining these two areas is their considerable interdependence in terms of journey-to-work, shopping flows, and all measured forms of spatial interchange. Further, the city boundaries are now only eight kilometres apart and both cities have special interest in planning the green belt area separating them which is currently administered by Somerset. Against these factors of common interest stand their marked contrast in size and character as two cities and their different planning problems. Redcliffe-Maud argues that 'the whole Bristol–Bath area has already become, in many respects, a single area for living, and it should form a single local government unit'. While the observation is inescapable, the conclusion is debatable. The dispute on this topic within the Commission itself is shown in a note of reservation which recommends that integration between Bristol and Bath should be handled at the provincial level and that the Bristol–Bath unit should be divided into two. Senior's minority report comes to a similar conclusion.

The second criterion introduces familiar notions of efficiencies of scale. It was argued that the new cohesive units must be large enough to provide local government services 'efficiently'. 'Large enough' was considered to be in the population band of 250,000 to 1,000,000. These limits are broadly defined and represent compromise figures for a range of local government services with very different size requirements. In practice it proved extremely difficult to obtain statistically convincing evidence on the economies of size, and harder still to define or agree a minimum threshold. The Home Office considered 500,000 the minimum population that would support an efficient police force, while the Department of Education and Science supported this threshold but were prepared to lower it to 300,000 in sparsely populated areas. Rather lower figures were given for local health and welfare authorities (200,000) and for child care services (250,000). Figure 3 shows how the new units measure up to these criteria and compares them with the existing county units and with the alternative system of units proposed by Senior.

The third and final criterion used in the delimitation of the new units was the present pattern. Wherever possible existing units and their boundaries, even at county level, were used as building blocks for the new units in order to retain common interests and traditional loyalties, to preserve the skill and momentum of existing local authorities, and to minimize change-over problems. It is clear that the investment and control systems of existing authorities have a long-term momentum; this cannot be immediately interrupted and diverted by central legislation but must necessarily be carried through by the new authorities. Parts of the old county boundaries are used both by the Redcliffe-Maud report and by Derek Senior. The persistence of the Somerset–Devon boundary, the south-east Wiltshire and the Gloucester boundaries in the proposals for the South-west suggest some interesting carry-overs from historical geography. Moreover, five of the six counties are retained, albeit in a reduced form.

What kind of overall characteristics do the sixty-one new units display? The data available for the units deserves a full analysis but some crude idea of characteristics displayed by the units can be derived from the relationships between people, area and potential local revenue described in the Redcliffe-Maud report. The contrast

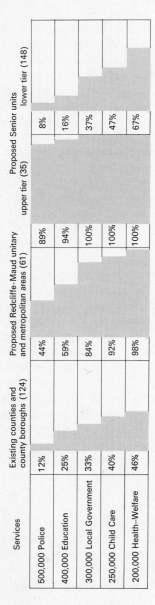

Figure 3

Services	Existing counties and county boroughs (124)	Proposed Redcliffe-Maud unitary and metropolitan areas (61)	Proposed Senior units upper tier (35)	Proposed Senior units lower tier (148)
500,000 Police	12%	44%	89%	8%
400,000 Education	25%	59%	94%	16%
300,000 Local Government	33%	84%	100%	37%
250,000 Child Care	40%	92%	100%	47%
200,000 Health–Welfare	46%	98%	100%	67%

between low-density rural units and high-density metropolitan units is vast. The former mostly have populations of less than half a million and have both low rateable value per capita and, predictably, low rateable value per hectare. They are typified by Northumberland with a population of 240,000 (declining to 238,000 by 1981) and a rateable value of only £32 per capita and around £15 per hectare (Figure 4).

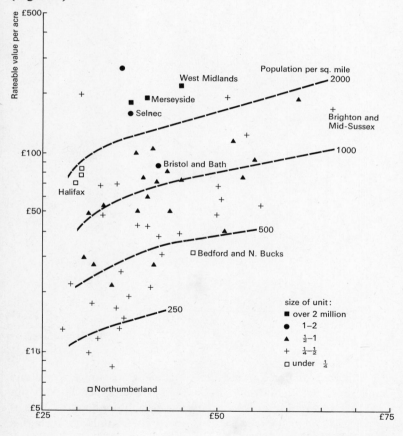

Figure 4

125

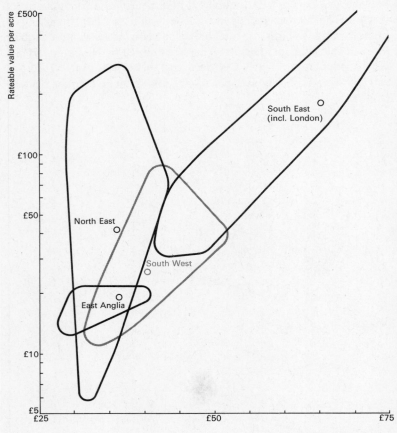

Figure 5

The high-density urbanized units include a mixture of large and small units with uniformly high rateable values per hectare but variable per capita values. Among the units with population densities of over 380 per square kilometre are units as unlike as Halifax (195,000 population with £28 per capita) and Brighton and Mid-Sussex (429,000 population with £66 per capita), as well as the three

126

metropolitan areas (the West Midlands, for example, has a population of 3,014,000 and a rateable value of £45 per capita).

This variability is one of the problems which will need coordination at the provincial level. Intra-regional contrasts, however, are much greater in some of the eight regions than in others. The five units of the North East Province cover a very wide range in per hectare characteristics but have common problems in low per capita rateable values. The distinctness of the small and compact East Anglian Province in relation to the expansive South East Province underlines the justness of the majority decision of the Redcliffe-Maud report to give the former separate provincial status. The South-west occupies a middle order position in Figure 5 with none of the acute urban renewal problems facing its northern neighbours.

In one sense, the Redcliffe-Maud report is a vindication for the arguments put forward by several geographers over the last two or three decades. The proposed units are explicitly based on an integration of town and country and on what the report calls the 'socio-geographic realities' of contemporary England. But in the continuing debate there remain some intriguing areas of geographic investigation and theory that remain relatively untapped.

First, little has been heard from research about the immensity of the region-building problem. If we take the simple task of grouping five counties into a set of regions we know that fifty-two groupings are possible. From this trivial level the number of possible combinations expands explosively. For ten counties it leaps to over a thousand possible groupings and for 124 counties – the problem facing Redcliffe-Maud with existing administrative counties and county boroughs – it soars to hundreds of billions of possibilities. Most of these solutions would be rejected out of hand but sample inspection of the more favourable suggest that there may be many thousands of 'acceptable' solutions to the problem tackled by the Royal Commission. Debate and controversy are natural outcomes both of the immensity of the problem and of the impossibility, at least with existing computing capacity, of demonstrating that an ideal situation has been achieved. Given this difficulty and, therefore, that the final answer may not yet have been found, there is some scope for geographic research. Computer programmes for finding optimum district boundaries have been widely used in the United States for defining electoral regions and could be adapted efficiently to work on boundary optimization problems in local government. The whole problem of regionalization may be approached through 'statistical taxonomy' and this method, established in geographic literature for more than a decade, might well be linked with tests such as Discriminant Analysis to develop and test alternative groupings.

Second, little has been heard about the effects of re-grouping on the 'successful' and 'unsuccessful' centres. For some small county towns such as Taunton in Somerset employment in local government is a substantial element in their employment structure, for others it is negligible. The distribution of administrative employment and its multiple effect on the local economy need further probing.

Third, the challenge of the future. The Redcliffe-Maud report includes estimates for population in 1981. Research on contemporary urbanization trends and on regional population forecasting models may suggest that the proposed structure has a longer term viability in some areas than in others. The likely need for adaptability suggests itself for further study.

Many other aspects demand fuller investigation. Some interesting work by the report on the perception of local community areas needs following up. How far is England moving towards what Berkeley planner Mel Webber has described as a 'non-place realm' where conventional distance becomes unimportant and rather random and apparently untidy arrangements of homes, jobs and facilities are highly efficient? To what extent are regions incidental by-products of a modernization process rooted in systems management and programme budgeting rather than end-products to be carefully optimized and re-fashioned? Along with the answers that Redcliffe-Maud proposes are a series of questions that will occupy the analysts in many disciplines for a generation.

References

Freeman, T. W., *Geography and Regional Administration*, Hutchinson, 1968.
Maass, A., *Area and Power: a theory of local government*, Free Press, 1969.
Mackintosh, J. P., *Devolution of Power*, Penguin Books, 1968.
Royal Commission on Local Government in England (The Redcliffe–Maud Report), HMSO (3 vols.), 1969.

Leisure and the Countryside:
the Example of the Dartmoor National Park

by C. Board, D. Brunsden, J. Gerrard, B. S. Morgan, C. D. Morley and J. B. Thornes

Recreation and associated leisure activities were once luxuries for the select few, but this is no longer the case. Social and economic progress have created an affluent and well-educated population able to seek and enjoy a wide range of leisure pursuits. An increasing number of people now wish to visit beautiful and interesting areas of the countryside, and this has led to intense pressures which have created planning problems of a new kind in the most popular areas. The effective management of people in the countryside and the threat of damage to the environment stand out as challenges which must be faced if the different uses for the countryside are to continue without undue friction.

The source of these new pressures is the affluent population of the urban area of Britain using cars for weekend recreation. Forty-five per cent of the population now has access to a car and uses it for extensive recreation travel. This pressure can only increase as the 14,800,000 vehicles of Britain in 1969 rise to an estimated 26,000,000 in the year 2000 (Figure 1).

The problem is accentuated by availability of both time and money to a wide section of the population. The working week will continue to shrink and leisure time, which people will seek to fill with interesting activities, will increase. Their ability to do this will be helped partly by the affluence of the society in which incomes are increasing and in which every one per cent increase in real income will probably be accompanied by a three per cent increase in real expenditure on leisure. People not only wish to enjoy leisure activities, they are now able to do so.

The areas of Britain which will be most affected by outdoor leisure are the National Parks, Areas of Outstanding Natural Beauty and of Great Landscape Value and those areas of agricultural land and forestry which are close to the main urban centres (Figure 2). With

129

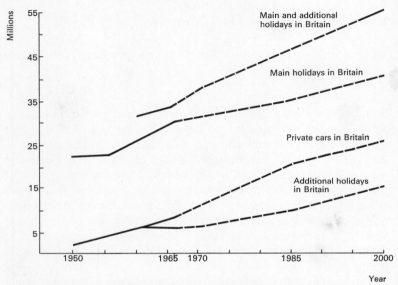

Figure 1 Trends in holidays and car ownership, with a forecast of what may be anticipated for A.D. 2000.

improved road communications and motorways, the numbers travelling will increase and they will be able to reach many of the remote areas of England and Wales on weekend trips.

Concern with this situation has been reflected in an increasing volume of published work on recreation, the Government White Paper *Leisure in the Countryside* (1966), and the Countryside Act, 1968, which set up the Countryside Commission and from which has arisen the concept of 'Country Parks'. Studies of recreation have been carried out by local authorities, government departments, and other research groups all wrestling with the need to evolve new principles of recreation management. Thus it is within the frame of the national demand for recreation and the background of previous work that the subject of this chapter – the Dartmoor National Park – must be considered.

Demand for leisure is particularly acute in South Devon where the Dartmoor National Park is close to the urban resident and

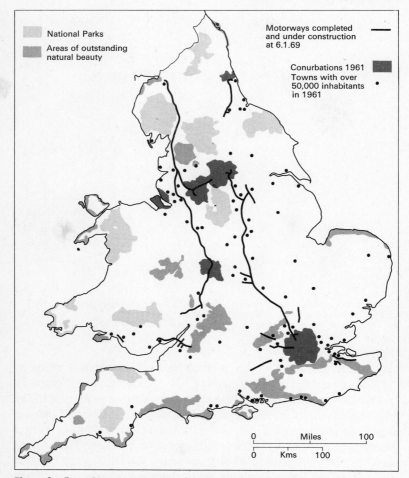

National Parks

Areas of outstanding
natural beauty

Motorways completed
and under construction
at 6.1.69

Conurbations 1961
Towns with over
50,000 inhabitants
in 1961

Miles   100

Kms   100

Figure 2   Even the remotest areas of outstanding beauty in England and
Wales are now accessible to day visitors.

summer tourist populations of Exeter, Torbay and Plymouth.
Approximately 500,000 residents and 200,000 visitors are within
48 kilometres of the National Park during the holiday season. A
survey in 1967 showed that more than 3,000,000 visits were made by

131

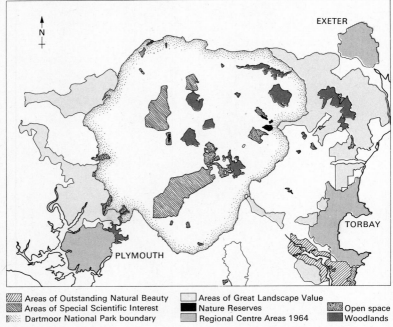

N

EXETER

TORBAY

PLYMOUTH

//// Areas of Outstanding Natural Beauty   ☐ Areas of Great Landscape Value
\\\\ Areas of Special Scientific Interest   ■ Nature Reserves   ▨ Open space
····· Dartmoor National Park boundary   ☐ Regional Centre Areas 1964   ■ Woodlands

Figure 3

day visitors during the year; in 1968 on peak Sundays as many as 55,000 visitors arrived in something like 15,000 vehicles (Figure 3).

The Dartmoor National Park has many diverse landscapes. The high moorlands of north and south Dartmoor are tracts of blanket bog, peat and granite covered with a characteristic flora of cotton grass, sphagnum, heather, whortleberry and bracken. These areas have no roads but have great attractions for the hiker, pony trekker, and naturalist. The high moorland to the north is used for military training, a use which is incompatible with the concept of the National Park. The ridges at lower elevations are usually occupied by common land and unenclosed moorland which, except where accessible by road, are only lightly used for recreation. These moorlands are grazed by sheep, cattle and ponies but in some areas this use competes with forestry, arable agriculture and mineral extraction. The same conflicts exist in the moorland valleys. Here the problem of competing land uses is more immediate where the demands for water storage and recreational use are much greater.

Some of the valleys are intensively used for recreation, especially those with wide flood plains or features of particular interest. The West Dart at Two Bridges, the Dart at Dartmeet, Newbridge and Spitchwick, the O Brook above Hexworthy and the Walla Brook at Riddon Brake, Pizwell and Babeny are heavily used by visitors. Wistman's Wood, an area of relict oak forest in the West Dart Valley some way from any road, has recently come under great pressure as a result of publicity both on television and in the press. Although the recreational and water storage uses of the moorland valleys conflict with other land uses, the two are complementary. Reservoirs create new beauty spots, as is shown by the large number of visitors to Burrator, Avon Dam, Fernworthy and Venford.

On gentler slopes and the moorland edge on the outskirts of the National Park additional problems are created by the presence of agricultural land. Perhaps the greatest pressure is felt at Widecombe and at the beauty spots of Lydford, Belstone, Fingle Bridge, Becka Falls, Shipley Bridge and Shaugh Bridge.

These contrasting landscapes present visitors with a range of recreational opportunities. An understanding of the way in which the choice between them is made is fundamental to an analysis of the recreational use of the National Park. Most visitors enter the National Park by car along the main roads at Moretonhampstead, Bovey Tracey, Ashburton, Buckfast and Tavistock. These roads all lead into the core area of the Park centred on the valley of the River Dart. Here the visitor has a choice of routes which will enable him to visit all of the main beauty spots or to undertake a sightseeing tour. Once the choice of route has been made further possibilities are presented by the kinds of places at which he may stop – whether common land, village centres, car parks or roadside verges.

The visitor will decide what he wishes to do from the range of options open to him at any site. The choice made will depend on the type of visitor, the natural and man-made resources, and the available access. Here conflict inevitably arises between the need to protect the environment and to make the benefits available to the public.

14. *Dartmoor provides the largest stretches of open land accessible to the half-million local residents and the West Country holiday makers. Scenic resources include wooded valleys, rocky outcrops, neat farm fields and rolling moorland. Below: Dart Valley.*

Recreational pressures are not spread evenly over the National Park. There are large areas of open moorland, woodland and agricultural land, which together probably make up well over 95 per cent of the total area but where the density of recreational use is low. The recreational activity of the great mass of the 3,000,000 yearly visitors is concentrated into a very small part. As a result certain beauty spots and roads are on occasion almost at, if not already beyond, capacity. It is this intensive recreational use that is of most concern.

Bearing in mind the nature of the problems already stated, a team of research workers has attempted to examine a part of the Dartmoor National Park with a view to: providing some of the information about recreation required for future analysis; examining the inter-relationships between various phenomena studied in relation to tourist activity; creating a dynamic model of the tourist system in inner Dartmoor. Many elaborate and very useful surveys have already been carried out in other parks, usually over prolonged periods and with special emphasis on certain aspects of tourist activity. The aim of this survey was to concentrate observations on a single peak day and to examine as many as possible of the characteristics of the recreational situation over this short period.

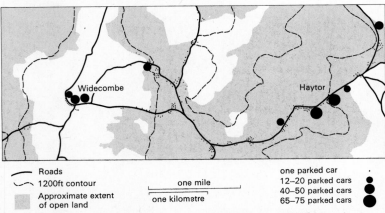

⌒ Roads	one parked car ·
⌒⌒ 1200ft contour	12–20 parked cars ●
Approximate extent of open land	40–50 parked cars ●
one mile	65–75 parked cars ●
one kilometre	

Figure 4 Some motorists who parked between Haytor and Widecombe on the afternoon of the survey congregated in car parks; others sought out solitary places. Most have easy access to open land unless they are visiting Widecombe.

In order to structure the analysis of such a complex situation the study area was conceived as a recreational system. This concept can be illustrated by the examination of a small section of the moor between Widecombe and Haytor. Figure 4 indicates the localities of all parked cars at the time of the aerial photography. There are four main components in the recreational situation: the major concentrations, in this case Widecombe and Haytor; minor concentrations at the road intersections and in quarries; connecting roads with associated verge parking; extensive areas of moorland or farmland.

The tourist system then consists of concentrations of visitors (nodes) and road networks (links) set within areas of varying character: the relationships between them are expressed in terms of flows of people. Researchers set out to examine a tourist system in inner Dartmoor (Figure 5) by making observations at all the major nodes, several minor nodes and three sets of links in the network, here called circuits.

The information collected related to three basic properties of the system – the characteristics of the visitors, the activities they carry out at these various places and the flows of visitors from outside the

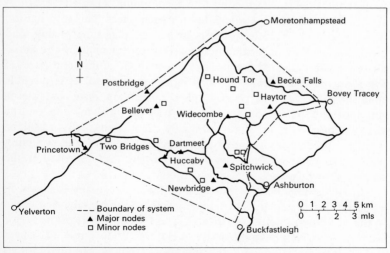

Figure 5   The road system and places in inner Dartmoor which were studied for the survey of the tourist system.

defined area and between various places within it. The characteristics of the visitors have been obtained by means of a carefully developed questionnaire and a team of 30 interviewers performed the task of interviewing. The occupants of cars were interviewed as they arrived at the various places in the system; the car driver was regarded as the spokesman for the group with which he was travelling. In all, some 750 groups were interviewed during the day. The second part of the operation was carried out by observers who circulated in the nodes at regular intervals counting the number of people engaged in specified activities. Finally, the observations of flows were made by recording car numbers at different places in the system, at car parks, on roadside verges and in minor nodes. For the car parks, the observers recorded, for each five-minute period, the registration numbers of arriving and departing cars; at other localities the total of all cars was observed at longer, less regular intervals. The operation extended from 11.00 to 19.00 hours with breaks for lunch and tea, in hot, sunny weather on Sunday, 10 August 1969.

In analysing the results of the traffic survey, registration numbers of vehicles using car parks at a selection of nodes and their times of arrival and departure were fed into a computer. Then the length of stay of each vehicle was calculated for each place. This information on trip patterns, vehicle numbers at a particular time of day, and lengths of stay at particular nodes was supplemented by the aerial survey which indicated the amount of use made of different parts of the road network during the photographing period. It is possible that the same car was photographed more than once, but this is unimportant, provided that the car was not still moving on the same section of road, a very unlikely event. Eventually it will be possible to compare intended trip patterns from the questionnaire, actual trip patterns from the vehicle survey, and the road traffic density shown by the aerial photographs.

The road traffic density indicated by the aerial survey is shown in Figure 6. Three salient features emerge. First, the heavily used roads in the south-east and the north-west. The former is part of the major scenic route which links the nodes of Haytor, Widecombe, Dartmeet and Huccaby; the latter is a through route from Moretonhampstead to Tavistock but also carries tourist traffic to Postbridge, Bellever and

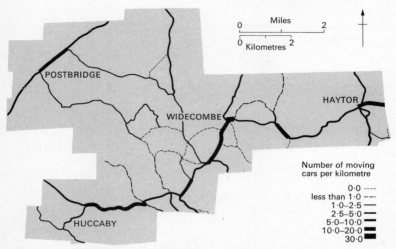

Figure 6   Many roads are almost deserted but popular signposted routes carry a high traffic density.

Princetown. Second, the survey shows the minor roads which link the two major routes and, third, the network of inner roads which are virtually unused.

Important questions arise from the survey such as to what extent the vehicles on the major roads are through traffic or tourist traffic? Do the nodes act as magnets for the traffic or are they used because they are on major roads? To what extent is the density of road traffic a function of the level of information available to the visitor in the form of signposting?

Figure 7 shows the total number of vehicles present at any one time and the turnover for three selected nodes. In addition to indicating the relative popularity of Huccaby when compared with Widecombe, it shows interesting differences between the three nodes. At Huccaby the number of arriving cars is persistently higher than the number leaving until about 16.30, after which the situation is completely reversed. At Widecombe the picture is rather similar but turnover is more rapid, whereas at Haytor cars arrive and depart regularly throughout the day, though there are still, in the early afternoon, more arriving than departing cars. All the car parks show

139

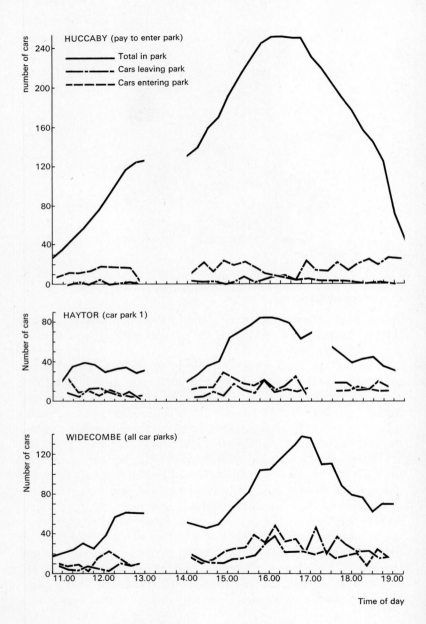

HUCCABY (pay to enter park)
number of cars

Total in park
Cars leaving park
Cars entering park

HAYTOR (car park 1)
Number of cars

WIDECOMBE (all car parks)
Number of cars

Time of day

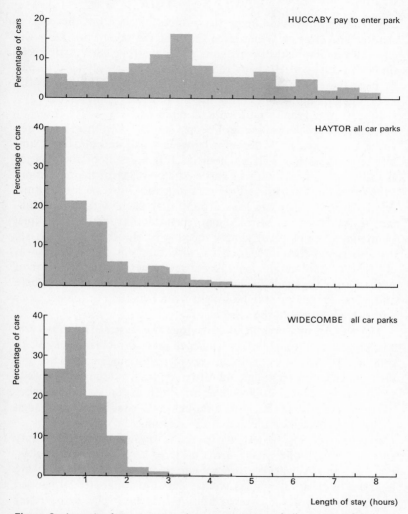

Figure 8   Length of stay expressed as a percentage of all cars stopping.

◀ Figure 7   Turnover and total numbers of vehicles in three selected places compared throughout the day.

a late afternoon maximum in the number of cars, but the peak is sharper and later at Widecombe than for the other two. Does the clear distinction between arriving and departing cars at different times of the day at Huccaby reflect simply that people have to pay to park there? Or does it reflect a fundamental difference in the demands, intentions and composition of visitors going there?

Finally, the graphs in Figure 8 represent lengths of stay. At Huccaby the greatest number of people stay between three and three and a half hours; at Widecombe between a half and one hour; and at Haytor less than half an hour. Is this a result of the type of activities in which the visitors participate? At Haytor they can climb to the rocks and return to their cars in a very short period of time. At Widecombe, they can look around the village and take refreshments. At Huccaby, visitors may spend longer periods of time, swimming, picnicking or simply relaxing by the river. If this is so, are different activities associated with different types of visitor, characteristics of the site including attractiveness, or the provision of natural and man-made facilities there? The answer to some of these and earlier questions may be sought from the study of the activities and characteristics of the visitors.

The pattern of recreational behaviour was assessed by observers who circulated through all parts of each node at regular intervals. In general, the relatively small numbers of visitors in the morning and the peak experienced in the mid-afternoon bear out the results of the traffic survey (Figure 9). Problems arising from congestion are more likely to occur in the afternoon although some sites are small enough to appear crowded by the end of the morning.

Four contrasting nodes, two riverside sites, a moorland beauty spot and a moorland village, are considered here. The riverside sites, Huccaby and Newbridge, are similar in many respects. Both are bounded by steep valley sides, so that views are dominated by wooded or sometimes bracken-covered hillsides. At both places the River Dart is crossed by an attractive, old stone bridge. Open land immediately adjacent to the river is a common feature of both sites and small-scale facilities – a toilet and shop or ice cream van – are available. Huccaby, the larger of the two, has two car parking areas. One, a field adjacent to the river, is private property with a 10 p charge

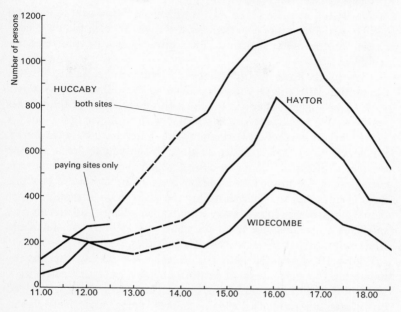

Figure 9   Even on a hot day most visitors arrive after lunch.

but the other, of much more limited size but with free parking, is among rocks and trees beside the river. At 16.30 hours 1,160 visitors were counted at Huccaby, 950 of whom were in the private car park. The other site, Newbridge, attracted no more than 350 people. At this smaller site the part nearest the river is barred to vehicles, but there is no charge for parking.

The moorland site, Haytor, is not so confined as either of the riverside sites. It has a clear focus in its twin pile of rocks which can be seen from many miles away, but all around is open land which is penetrated by the more adventurous walkers. The rocks themselves are easily accessible from a free hard-core car park on the nearby road. Along much of the road, however, lie long stretches of low verges and even wider areas of grass onto which cars may be easily driven. All of these places have good views of the rocks and direct paths up to them. Eight hundred and fifty visitors were present in the

143

area at 16.00. Because of the way in which open land next to the road can be used even more cars than were actually there could have been parked on the site at that time. Two refreshment caravans regularly serve the site.

The fourth node is the village of Widecombe, famed for its association with the Devonshire folk-song. The *Dartmoor National Park Guide* suggests that it is the most commercialized of the villages and that 'the intelligent visitor will not wish to linger in it', but for those who do the facilities are abundant. Three hard-core car parks, for which no charge is made, lie close to the village green and the cluster of historic, granite buildings which include a church, 'the cathedral of the moor'. In addition there is limited street parking. Several cafés and souvenir shops are the other main attractions since there is little open ground, away from traffic, where children can play safely. A short distance from the centre of Widecombe, farmland effectively restricts the activities of all visitors.

Figure 10 shows the activities at each site during the day by indicating the percentage of visitors engaged in water activities – swimming, paddling, scrambling on river boulders, fishing; engaged in other active pursuits – playing games, flying model aeroplanes, etc.; using facilities such as cafés and refreshment caravans; staying in or near their cars; engaged in other activities such as picnicking, strolling, sightseeing or sunbathing. At Haytor the number on the rocks and paths leading up to them was also counted.

Water activities were less popular at Newbridge than at Huccaby where the river was a focus for 4 in every 10 visitors between 15.30 and 16.00. As water activities became more important during the afternoon, at both sites other active pursuits, which were most popular in the morning and late afternoon, declined.

Nevertheless, at any one time, less than half of the visitors were involved in any sort of active recreation at Huccaby and Newbridge. At the other two sites however, even fewer participate in active recreation. In Widecombe the negligible proportions reflect the small scope for such activities in a situation where buildings and fairly busy streets replace open grass. More surprisingly at Haytor, where there is ample opportunity for games and the like, comparatively few were taking part in these pursuits. Throughout most of the day the rocks and the paths up to them consistently attracted between 10 and 25 per cent of all visitors. At the same time a considerable proportion stay in their cars. This relates to the suggestions derived from the analysis of the traffic survey. Two underlying trends may be detected in the pattern at Haytor. First, the largest proportion of visitors staying in or near their cars occurs in the afternoon when picnicking is very common especially in the grassed parking areas. Second, the

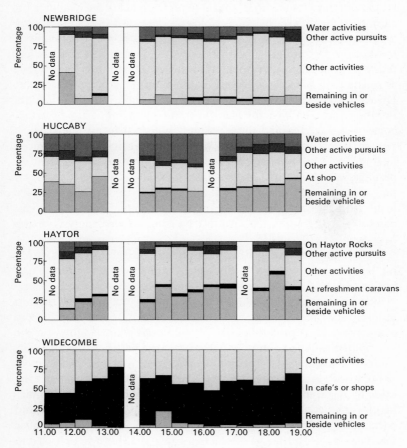

Figure 10   Activities at four varied sites.

Time of day

rocks and their approaches reach peaks of popularity early and late in the day. As Haytor lies on a scenic route close to the edge of Dartmoor this might indicate that short term visitors climb the rocks for a view at the beginning or end of a composite trip.

It is clear that at Widecombe the tourist is amply provided with facilities for refreshment and shopping and that these are well used, with peak use not unexpectedly occurring at midday and at tea-time. At the other nodes facilities for buying refreshments are available on a limited scale, but the extent to which they are used varies. At Haytor and Newbridge the refreshment caravans are popular throughout most of the day, but at Huccaby the small shop attracts relatively few of the large number of visitors to the site. At Haytor it is known that a substantial number of tourists make short stops, whereas at Huccaby they stay for longer periods. It is possible that these visitors use their cars as a base for picnicking and changing. They probably come well prepared and therefore may not need to use the shop to any great extent. If the visitors were local in origin they are more likely to have been prepared for a full scale family picnic – a feature perhaps less typical of holiday-makers. Analysis of car registration numbers supports this idea: one third of the cars at Huccaby are local, from Devon, whereas only about one tenth are local at Widecombe. Further confirmation must be sought from analysis of the questionnaire.

Preliminary analysis of the questionnaire described here is based on the completed questionnaires from four nodes – Widecombe, Postbridge, Bellever and Spitchwick – and the Hound Tor circuit. These results are derived from samples of groups at these places so that no generalizations can be made with absolute certainty. Nonetheless, there is at least a 20: 1 probability that the account which follows on the basis of the sample accurately reflects the true patterns of behaviour.

One of the striking features to emerge is that the places most popular with local residents visiting Dartmoor for the day are not the same as those most frequented by holiday-makers. This has fundamental implications in terms of length of stay, trip structure and patterns of activity. At Spitchwick more than 90 per cent of those interviewed lived within 48 kilometres and in the Hound Tor area and at Bellever more than three-quarters of those interviewed were local visitors; on the other hand, at Postbridge and Widecombe just over half of those interviewed lived more than 48 kilometres away (Figure 11).

Two possible reasons can be advanced to explain these contrasts. Long distance visitors generally have recreational requirements different from those of local residents. Long distance visitors are less informed about Dartmoor and as a result frequent the better known, more accessible places of interest.

The first possibility is that long distance visitors are mainly concerned with seeing Dartmoor, whereas the local visitors are not

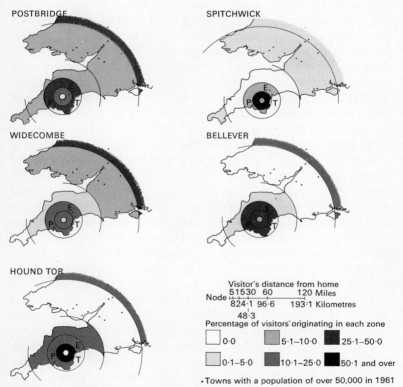

Figure 11   Selection of venue is influenced by local knowledge.

147

concerned so much with touring as with open-air recreation, be it active, swimming or walking, or passive, relaxing and enjoying the sun in pleasant surroundings. It may be argued that Bellever and Spitchwick, which are both situated on the River Dart, away from main roads, and the Hound Tor area, where people can easily drive off the road and relax, best suit the needs of the local population. On the other hand, Widecombe and Postbridge, with its well preserved clapper bridge, have obvious attractions for the sightseer.

Analysis of the questionnaire data on intended activities is only at a preliminary stage and no evidence can be presented to show that long distance visitors and local residents have different recreational aims which take them to different nodes. However, evidence is available concerning activities at the nodes themselves which by inference goes a long way to suggest that there is a difference. At Widecombe, the node with the greatest percentage of long-distance visitors, three-quarters of those interviewed intended to do some sightseeing while no one was there for active recreation; at Spitchwick, the node with the greatest percentage of local visitors, more than three-quarters of respondents intended to carry on some form of active recreation during their stay, mostly swimming, and 7 out of 10 intended to spend part of their time just relaxing.

In addition, there is strong evidence that the long distance visitor stops at more places than the local resident. Only 10 per cent of the former group compared with nearly 50 per cent of locals stopped once only. This is reflected in the fact that 90 per cent of the persons at Widecombe had stopped or intended to stop again while 54 per cent of visitors to Spitchwick intended to spend their whole time there. It seems probable then that the distance visitors live from Dartmoor affects their choice of destination as a result of their different recreational demands.

However, this does not provide the complete answer. The problem can best be illustrated with reference to Postbridge and Bellever. These nodes are situated on the East Dart River only a mile apart and are both sited by clapper bridges; they differ in that Bellever is more secluded and the starting point of a Forestry Commission Nature Trail, while Postbridge is situated on one of the main routes across Dartmoor and is served by a café and hotel. The intended activities at these two nodes differ tremendously: 57 per cent of respondents at Postbridge intended to look at the view, 30 per cent actually mentioning the clapper bridge and 17 per cent intending to photograph it, and only 20 per cent came for general open-air recreation. At Bellever, only 9 per cent intended to do any sightseeing, nobody mentioning the clapper bridge, while half intended to take part in active pursuits and half to relax or picnic. Trip structure, particularly of groups of long distance visitors, cannot be understood purely in terms of recreational demands. The legend surrounding Widecombe makes it unique but there are many clapper bridges, many tors, many quaint villages on Dartmoor. The information level of the group largely determines which ones are visited. Postbridge, the clapper bridge the guide books describe and the most accessible, is inundated with sightseers, while at Bellever the clapper bridge goes almost unnoticed.

.Information level is assessed in two ways on the questionnaire: first, by a series of questions 'What are the following places famous for?'; second, by asking the driver to recognize places shown on a series of photographs of graded difficulty. One point is awarded for a right answer and the total possible score is 14 points. There is, as suggested, a strong relationship between the distance visitors live from Dartmoor and their knowledge about the moor; those visitors from more than 48 kilometres had an average information score of 3·76 compared with 6·30 for local residents. Those visitors living outside south-western England not only visit Dartmoor relatively infrequently and so learn little at first hand but also do not have the opportunity to acquire information about the National Park from the regional news media. Groups visiting the four nodes and the Hound Tor area have different information scores: the average information score is lowest at those places visited by the greatest number of long distance visitors. Thus, at Widecombe the average score for visitors is 4·91, at Postbridge 4·05, while at Bellever it is 6·88, at Spitchwick 5·86 and in the Hound Tor area 5·51.

In general the lower information scores of the long distance visitors seem, at least in part, to explain their greater concentration at Postbridge and Widecombe. It is those few with the higher information scores who stray from well-known routes, to visit places such as Bellever and the Hound Tor area. The average information score for visitors from more than 48 kilometres is 5·25 at Bellever and 5·08 in the Hound Tor area, compared with 3·49 at Widecombe and 2·79 at Postbridge. Only three long-distance visitors were interviewed at Spitchwick so that their mean information score (4·0) has little significance. The observed difference in group origin can be explained only in terms of the complex interaction of the differing recreational demands of these groups and their knowledge of Dartmoor – an analysis which is beyond the scope of this chapter.

There are two major problems to be faced if our national parks are to be able to handle the expected increase in the number of visitors. These are the measurement of capacity and the choice of an appropriate solution to over-capacity use. Road congestion in a national park like Dartmoor occurs at weekends and holidays. The destination of much of this traffic is the tourist nodes which become congested when their capacity is exceeded. Capacity may be assessed in three ways. Physical capacity is the number of vehicles and people that can actually get into an area. Ecological capacity is the point at which real damage is done to the physical environment by too many people or misuse of land. Psychological capacity is the point at which the node is considered too crowded by the visitor himself, with the result that he moves on. A major task is to measure these levels before assessing the optimum use of the national park's recreation space.

The question of optimum use of resources of limited occurrence raises the second major problem – that of management as a solution to congestion. Three broadly different strategies are open. In each, information available to the public is a vitally important component.

STRATEGY ONE. This is the maintenance of the *status quo*. Existing levels of information about the Park, its beauty spots, historical sites and natural monuments remain as at present, while the Park environment is preserved in its present form. The most likely effect of this will be increasing congestion in the better known places and on the roads linking them.

STRATEGY TWO. Information levels are maintained as at present but the environment is modified to ease the present congestion. This could involve widening roads, enlarging car parks and providing more toilets and picnic sites, all of which would by some degree alter the present landscape.

STRATEGY THREE. The environment is left essentially unchanged but the information available to visitors and potential visitors is manipulated. Existing information is of two kinds, that published on maps, in guidebooks and leaflets and that appearing on signposts and guideposts. The National Park Information Centre at Two Bridges provides published information to callers. By careful selection of information in leaflets or on signposts it would be possible to direct visitors to selected places.

The method by which management of resources could be carried out is crucial. The present work of the County Council, National Parks Committee, wardens and voluntary wardens, considering their limited financial resources, is admirable, but any large increase in the number of visitors will make a reconsideration of the position imperative. It might become desirable for the Park to be managed as a separate entity with its own finances, a park director, an educational officer and a fully qualified management team.

Finally, it must not be forgotten that the national park is the home and livelihood of residents engaged in farming, forestry or other forms of land management not primarily concerned with recreation or with the concept of national parks. The impact of the leisure explosion on these people is severe and if something is done to alleviate the position for tourists, it should not be done without the full cooperation of the residents.

We end therefore with a series of problems and questions. The answers to the questions and solutions of the problems depend on research and planning. The successful application of policies which will be developed may, we hope, provide us with a better Dartmoor in the future and be a guide to policy decisions elsewhere.

References

Brunsden, D., *Dartmoor*, Geographical Association. British Landscape through Maps, 1968.

Burton, T. L., and Wibberley, G. P., *Outdoor Recreation in the British Countryside*, Wye College, Studies in Rural Land Use, Report No. 5, 1965.

Dartmoor, National Parks Guide No. 1, HMSO, 1957.

Resources for Britain's Future

United Kingdom Government, *Countryside Act, 1968*, HMSO, 1968.
United Kingdom Government, *Leisure in the Countryside, England and Wales*, Cmnd 2928, HMSO, 1966.

Acknowledgements

The Joint School Survey of the Dartmoor National Park was undertaken by six geographers from King's College London and the London School of Economics and sixty helpers for the day of the survey. The project was backed by the *Geographical Magazine* and supported by financial and other assistance from Devon County Council, Paul Cadbury, Fairey Surveys, the British Broadcasting Corporation and the geography departments of King's College, L.S.E. and the University of Exeter. The survey would not have been possible without the cooperation and help of local residents, landowners and holiday makers.

The Emerging Prospect

Britain on the Brink of Europe

by Michael Wise

The European Economic Community formally agreed in 1970 to open membership negotiations with the United Kingdom, Denmark, Ireland, and Norway who submitted their applications in 1967. The negotiation period is likely to last for some time, a period which will also see further changes in the organization of the Community itself. By 1973 or at least by the middle of the decade, Britain may be fully a member of the European Community and thus become a part of what is already forming a major economic region on the world map.

At present, the area of the Community is 1,167,500 square kilometres, nearly five times that of the UK; in 1968 its population was 186,000,000, compared with our own 55,000,000; its steel production in the same year was 98,000,000 tons, whilst the UK produced 26,000,000. The Community has been one of the faster growing major economic regions of the world: between 1958 and 1966 the combined gross product of the six member countries increased by 51 per cent – the USA and the UK meanwhile recorded increases of 45 per cent and 30 per cent respectively. It is a great trading region: trade between the members of the Community more than tripled between 1958 and 1966, and trade with the rest of the world also rose rapidly. Not all these increases are due directly to the establishment of the Community, but it seems clear that the removal of trade barriers and the gradual move from a national to a European market framework have been effective stimulants. The ideal situation will be reached when merchandise, capital and people can move freely as between places in a single market. This is still some way off but the practical re-opening of the question of Britain's entry should be causing us to ask what changes are necessary in our policies and economic structure to enable us to align smoothly and efficiently

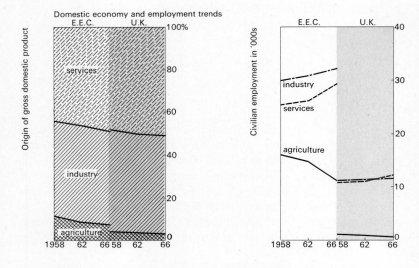

Domestic economy and employment trends

with Europe. We should also be considering the geographical implications of those changes. How will they affect particular industries and regions?

We should guard against the temptation to visualize revolutionary changes in Britain's economic geography occurring in a few dramatic years as a direct result of entry into the Common Market. Geographical patterns of social and economic activity are constantly changing: the entry of Britain into the Community will add a new set of circumstances to the factors influencing these changes. Moreover, there is usually a time lag between economic or political change and the appearance of geographical consequences.

Changes in the location of industrial plant, commercial premises, homes and schools are not achieved in a moment. It will take time for concerns to evaluate the scope of the new opportunities or the strength of the new handicaps and to adjust accordingly. But, while we should not over-estimate the rate at which geographical change may take place following entry, we should remember that some concerns may already be anticipating future market and supply situations and making their adjustments in advance.

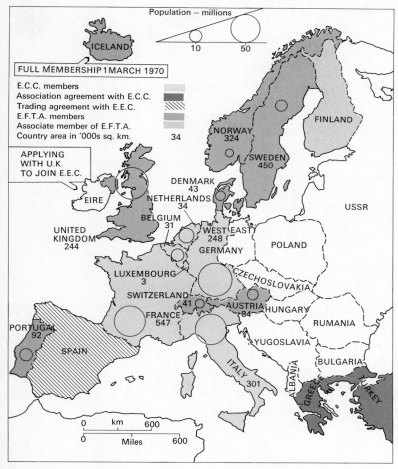

Figure 2

The economic advantages of the Common Market stem, in the first place, from its size. The elimination of internal tariffs (largely achieved in 1969) and the adoption of common policies for transport have tended to lead to an increase in internal trade and to an increase in competition between firms and areas in the member countries.

157

Productive forces in the different areas will tend to concentrate on those commodities for which they possess comparative advantages. This, again, should lead to an increase in economic specialization by areas. The larger markets open to low cost producers will enable them to increase their scale of output, so securing economies of large scale production. One result of this may be a growth in the number of large-scale producing units and organizations. There will be amalgamations of existing companies. Firms will choose locations carefully with a view to securing the best market areas for their products. Locations at or near junction points on the developing system of main air, road and rail communications linking industrial areas and seaports will tend to increase in relative importance.

In indicating the possibility for the growth of large concerns, we should not overlook the opportunities for manufacturers at medium and small scales. These perhaps will be greatest in areas where advantages can be obtained by a concentration of manufacturers engaged in similar or in 'linked' processes. Large firms tend to rely on small firms for the supply of specialized components. Small firms also have particular roles in supplying local needs, especially of con-

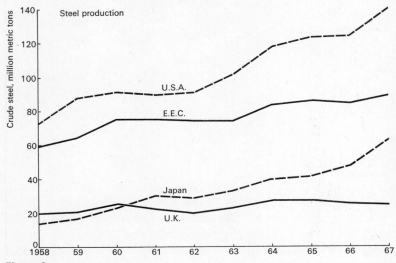

Figure 3

sumer goods and services. As there will not be an immediate Europeanization of all tastes and habits, entry into the European Community will not spell the beginning of the end for small enterprises: to the contrary, for efficient enterprises in most industries a greater range of opportunities for success should be opened up.

What effect will entry into the Community have on Britain's principal industries? It is, of course, industrial Britain that stands to gain most from membership of the European Community. In recent years many countries have developed the kind of industries on which much of our former industrial prosperity was founded, such as cotton textiles and mechanical engineering. Britain meanwhile has been moving into a stronger position in products that are more sophisticated technically and require heavy capital backing. Usually such products need to be produced on a large scale, for example man-made fibres, and so a substantial market which is close at hand is essential. Thus, large-scale, science based industries such as the manufacture of electronics, chemicals, and computers should benefit greatly. So, too, should those industries which already have established markets in west European countries. In 1958, 13·9 per cent of our exports went to EEC countries: since 1962 the EEC share has been approximately one-fifth (Figure 4).

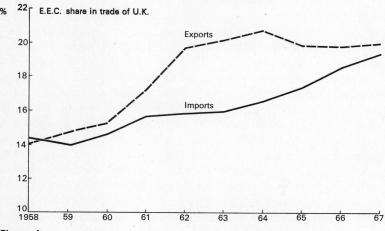

Figure 4

Several attempts have been made to predict which manufacturing industries will best stand the test of increased competition and will achieve larger markets in Europe. Some years ago an assessment was made based on the export success of industries in the period 1953–5 to 1960–62 (Balassa, 1965; Wells, 1966). Amongst the group of manufactures likely to prosper were tractors, power generating machinery, paint and varnish, commercial vehicles, woollen fabrics, synthetic dyestuffs, leather, and rubber tyres. In a more doubtful category were industries such as paper articles, rubber manufacturing excluding tyres, other machinery, and tubing. A further group including organic chemicals, office machinery, iron and steel bars, cotton fabrics, footwear, clothing, and scientific instruments had rather less hopeful prospects.

A review published in the *Economist*, 19 November 1966, forecast success for chemicals, especially petro-chemicals, electronics, heavy electrical engineering including electrical generating equipment, mass produced clothing and rainwear, and food products. Steel, popular type motor cars, mechanical engineering, and textiles, with some exceptions like knitwear, seemed to have more doubtful prospects.

A very recent attempt (Institute of Directors, 1969) to draw up a balance sheet of advantages and disadvantages ends with three groups of industries: 'gainers' include electronics, chemicals, chemical, electrical and mechanical engineering, and the 'aerospace' industries; 'moderate gainers' include motor manufacturing, shipbuilding, and textiles; 'possible losers' are scientific instruments, paper, footwear, food and confectionery.

The estimates show both similarities and differences. It is difficult to calculate not only how British industries will compete in Europe but also how well European firms will compete in Britain. There are no final answers at this stage. Whatever the industrial group, much will depend on the efficiency of the firm, the success of its commercial policy, and the strength of its technical backing. In the long run the industries likely to succeed most are those that are science based, with a high ratio of capital to output, and of sufficient scale of organization, or sufficiently enterprising, to be able to take advantage of the greatly increased potential market. Present efforts to improve the structure of British industry will doubtless continue.

The case of agriculture raises very controversial questions: indeed, some believe that the agricultural policy adopted by the Community creates so many problems as to cast doubt on the wisdom of our application to join. The method of price support adopted in Britain through the system of guaranteed minimum prices and deficiency payments would eventually disappear as we adjusted to the European system which, with some safeguards, supports farm incomes through a market price system with levies or duties against imports from non-member countries. The Community system does not provide the same degree of certainty of return to farmers as does our own. Britain is arguing for some changes in present policies, for a transitional period of adjustment, and for special arrangements for important sectors of Commonwealth trade. In this latter category the sugar producing countries and New Zealand, whose economy depends greatly on agricultural exports to Britain, could be very seriously affected. As a substantial importer of food, Britain would be required to make a large contribution to the costs of the common agricultural policy by paying into the central fund proceeds of levies on the imports of farm products and also by making direct budgetary contributions.

While improvements have been recorded in farm output and productivity in the Community, it is still true that too many people are working too many small farms. Of the total EEC workforce, agriculture employs 14 per cent, compared with about 3 per cent in Britain. In some countries, notably France, there is a need for a continued re-structuring of farming. Indeed, the executive body of the Common Market, the European Commission, has recently proposed a ten-year reform plan to modernize the existing small farm enterprises into much larger production units.

How would the generally more efficient British farmers fare with prices at the European level but faced with competition from their European counterparts? Producers of wheat, barley and rye should earn higher prices. Beef producers should be in a favourable position. The situation of milk producers is not easy to forecast but may not greatly change. Doubts have been expressed about the future circumstances of producers of wool, potatoes, mutton and lamb, though changes in the Community's arrangements may ease the uncertainty.

161

More difficult situations have been forecast for egg producers and especially for the horticultural industry, which would lose its duty protection against Community producers. Individual farmers' experience would undoubtedly reflect the efficiency of their own enterprises. A good deal of action has also been taken in Britain to improve farm structure and to prepare the horticultural industry for the strains of possible entry. It is a mixed picture. While the agricultural industry as a whole could gain, there will be serious problems for some sectors, some areas, and for some farmers.

Britain's servicing industries seem likely to gain from entering the Community. Great scope exists for the growth of the holiday and travel industries in Europe and for attracting European tourists to Britain: investment in suitable hotel and recreational facilities could prove rewarding. The City of London could well attract more Continental business in banking and insurance. More and more posts of the kind advertised in today's newspapers as 'Consultant to Europe' will become available – a necessary qualification for them seems to be fluency in at least one European language. Will the study of Europe – its history, geography, literature and languages – attain new emphasis in our schools, colleges of further education and universities?

Free movement of men and women throughout the Community is, of course, a general principle, as is freedom of the citizens of the Community to take up work of many, though not of all, kinds in any member country. National governments have safeguards over the restriction of immigration should an influx of workers threaten the living standards and working conditions of workers already employed in an area. The indications are that increased freedom of movement is likely to prove possible especially for professional, skilled and scientific personnel, and again the implications for education and for occupational training are not inconsiderable.

As will have been realized, the incidence of economic change will fall unequally. Areas whose industries stand to prosper will gain, others will decline. Many agricultural regions in Europe may lose half their present farming populations during the 1970s. For reasons quite unconnected with the working of the European Community, regional fortunes rise and fall.

Regional policy has proved to be a subject on which all member countries have been most jealous of their rights. Countries have been opposed to intervention by the Commission in their local affairs. In 1969 the Commission defined its attitude to this situation by emphasizing that regional policies remain the responsibility of member countries: the Commission's role is seen as one of coordination, supplementing what the countries themselves are doing. Regional financial aid, it is stated, 'is most effective when accompanied by the necessary infra-structures, concentrated on industrial growth points, granted to sound enterprises which will have a strong impact on demand in the area, applied temporarily, proportional to the seriousness of regional problems, and allocated under regional programmes'. The Commission has proposed to review annually the situation in problem areas, to set up a permanent committee on regional development and to establish a fund from which regional development programmes could be assisted.

While some achievements may be recorded, as for example the assistance given to the 'pole of growth' in southern Italy, it is difficult to estimate how effective this policy for regional development may prove to be. Britain, on the other hand, has a long-standing and effective regional policy, including measures both of control and of incentive, designed to encourage regional development in areas in which as much as 20 per cent of its population live. How far will it be possible to maintain these measures while adhering also to the principles under which the European Community operates? Commenting recently on this question McCrone (1969) has indicated a problem that could cause difficulty arising from the long-standing use of controls, such as the Industrial Development Certificate, in British town and country planning. The use of such controls is far more limited in the Community and, he points out, there is the danger that the use of such a method in a European context 'may seriously backfire'. The refusal of permission to develop in, say, south-east England for the purpose of diverting an activity to a development area in Britain might have the effect of convincing the firm that it should go elsewhere, say 'to Rotterdam or Antwerp, and yet serve the same market'.

Writing in 1963 I ventured the conclusion that the operation of the

Common Market 'will add strength to the existing tendency towards the growth of regional concentrations of population and employment in Western Europe', leading to a heightening of the contrasts between the actively developing and the less prosperous areas (Wise, 1963). McCrone in 1969 came to a similar view: 'there is a danger that the regional problems would be aggravated by economic union'. For Great Britain, advantages would tend to accrue to the great concentrations in the south-east and the Midlands: the disadvantages would tend to be felt in the more peripheral areas of the west.

Clearly, Britain with experience of regional policies since 1946 has much to contribute to the formation of an effective regional policy for Europe. Within Britain the tendency might possibly be for some decrease in emphasis on the 'control' aspects of regional policy, and some increase in emphasis upon 'growth point' or 'development pole' concepts. These involve calculated and coordinated policies of investment in selected areas to endow them with improved accessibility, new environments, improved services, and thus improved locational prospects.

If our entry into the European Community is followed in a few years by the opening of the Channel Tunnel, British roads and railways will become part of a Community-wide transport network. There will be an even greater emphasis on the efficiency of the Channel crossings and on the improvement of road and rail links to crossing points. The Minister of Transport's provisional scheme for the 1970s and 1980s includes 'strategy routes' from London to the Channel ports and to Harwich. Roads to by-pass London on the south and west are planned: there may also be a need for a strategy route by-passing London on the east, downstream of the city, with a new Thames crossing by bridge or tunnel and connecting with routes to East Anglia and to the Midlands. Indeed, entry into the European Community might well bring about in Britain an increased awareness of west–east routes, for example to Humberside and to the ports on the Firth of Forth.

Lastly, some attention should be given to the implications for the political geography of Britain of entry into Europe. Geographers have tended to emphasize the insularity and individuality of Britain. Insularity has been regarded as a source of strength. Mackinder (1902), writing of Britain *of* Europe, yet not *in* Europe', saw her as free to devote resources, drawn ultimately from the continent, to the expansion of influence and trade across the oceans. More recently, Watson (1964) has argued that 'insularity is thus at the basis of British individuality – so much that many British scarcely have the sense of being European and it is now taking a great adjustment on their part to think in European terms'.

Much of the argument about Britain's entry has focused on the economic advantages and disadvantages. Yet the political implications must not be overlooked. The ultimate aim is for 'an ever-closer union between the European peoples' towards which the economic agreements are first steps. An institutional framework has been established with the Commission whose fourteen members are pledged to independence of national interests, and there is at least the embryo of a European 'parliament'. True, the Council of Ministers, whose members directly represent member governments, takes final policy decisions, though these are based on proposals from the Commission. There is also a Court of Justice to decide whether acts of the various institutions of the Community and of the member governments are compatible with the Treaties. The Community's economic policies, in any case, touch on many aspects of the internal policies of the member countries and must inevitably involve some surrender of national sovereignty in the interest of the Community. While the idea of the political as well as the economic unity of Europe is still only a distant prospect we should now begin to consider the question: 'How far are we prepared to become part of political Europe as well as of economic Europe?'

References

Balassa, B., 'Trade Liberalisation and "Revealed" Comparative Advantage', *The Manchester School of Economic and Social Studies*, XXXIII, May 1965, pp. 99–124.
Bird, J., 'Seaports and the European Economic Community', *Geographical Journal*, 133, September 1967, pp. 302–27.
Chisholm, M., 'The Common Market and British Manufacturing Industry and Transport', *Journal of the Town Planning Institute*, xlviii, January 1962, pp. 10–13.

Clark, C., Wilson, F., and Bradley, J., 'Industrial Location and Economic Potential in Western Europe, *Regional Studies*, 3, 1969, pp. 197–212.

European Community Information Service, Community Topics:
28, *The Common Agricultural Policy*, 1967.
33, *Regional Policy in an Integrated Europe*, 1969.

European Economic Community, Secretariat General of the Commission, *Memorandum on Regional Policy in the Community*, Supplement to Bulletin No. 12, 1969.
Memorandum on the Reform of Agriculture in the EEC, 1969.

Liesner, H. H., 'The European Common Market and British Industry', *Advancement of Science*, 55, 1957, pp. 215–27.

Lind, H., *Regional Policy in Britain and the Six*, and Flockton, C., *Community Regional Policy*, Chatham House/PEP European Series No. 15, 1970.

McCrone, G., *Regional Policy in Britain*, Allen & Unwin, 1969.

Mackinder, H. J., *Britain and the British Seas*, Heinemann, 1902.

New Zealand Monetary and Economic Council, *New Zealand and an Enlarged EEC*, 1970.

Parker, G., *The Logic of Unity*, Longman, 1968.

United Kingdom Government, *Britain and the European Communities: an economic assessment*, HMSO, Cmnd 4289, 1970.

Warley, T. K., *Agriculture: the cost of joining the Common Market*, PEP, April 1967.

Watson, J. W., 'The Individuality of Britain', in J. W. Watson and J. B. Sissons, *The British Isles*, Nelson, 1964.

Wells, S., *Trade Policies for Britain*, OUP, 1966.

Wise, M. J., 'The Common Market and the Changing Geography of Europe', *Geography*, xlviii, April 1963, pp. 129–38.

Wise, M. J., 'The Impact of a Channel Tunnel on the Planning of South-Eastern England', *Geographical Journal*, 131, June 1965, pp. 167–85.

Since this paper was written, negotiations between Britain and the EEC have resulted in agreement on major issues of substance. The agreements are set out in the White Paper, *The United Kingdom and the European Communities*, Cmnd. 4715, July 1971. On the question of the effects of entry on manufacturing industries, a further important source should be consulted, namely S. S. Han and H. H. Liesner, *Britain and the Common Market: the Effect of Entry on the Pattern of Manufacturing Production*, University of Cambridge, Department of Applied Economics, Occasional Paper 27, CUP, 1971.

Britain 2000: Speculations on the Future Society

by Peter Hall

The most important British resource, in the future even more than in the past, will be the British population. How many more of us there will be is a matter of doubt: after years of jacking up his future projections of the British population, the Registrar General is now jacking them down again. But the present expectation is that there will be a 15,000,000 gain up to the end of the century, taking us from the present 55,000,000 to 70,000,000 around the year 2000.

There is a real danger of being misled by the ecologists as to the results. Population growth has its bad effects, as Malthus first reminded us, when it outstrips the growth of resources. Looking at the situation in India, one can see the point; looking at Britain, one can see its irrelevance. With every mouth God sends a pair of hands; more relevantly in present conditions, He also sends a brain. An increasing population, in an advanced industrial country like Britain, is a younger, better educated, better trained, more adaptable population. It is more capable of taking innovative decisions in production and marketing. The very fact of population growth means an expanding home market, and a climate of business optimism. The market will be relatively young, and will create new demands, which young extrepreneurs will exploit and then sell to the world. If Britain had not possessed a rapidly rising population in the last decade, it is less likely that we would have developed the Beatles, or Mary Quant. And our balance of payments would have been the poorer.

Population growth, of course, has its problems – or rather challenges. A few pop stars blossom without much formal training; but by and large, youth needs education and training to exploit its talents. So an increasing proportion of the gross national product must go into education, which becomes the most important single long-term investment. There is a problem of allocating resources,

167

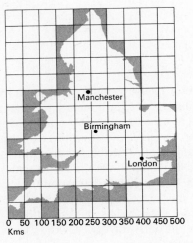

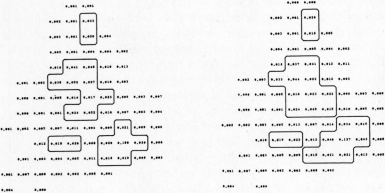

Figure 1 (Top) Map of England with a 50 × 50 km grid, the basis for the population projections by Lionel March. (Bottom left) A computer print-out of the 1961 population distribution for this grid. Areas with over 0.015 per 1,000 (1.5% of) the total population – the main concentrations – are outlined. (Bottom right) The computer projection of the year 2011. The main masses in the Midlands and the south have grown and spread.

which is compounded because the numbers of the very old are growing too – a result of high birth rates in Victorian and Edwardian times.

For the geographer, rising population also means problems of space. There is first the crude equation: people versus land. Here, it is vital to get the situation into historical perspective. The most careful calculations on the subject, by Best (1964), indicate that in 1900 about 5 per cent of England and Wales was built over by all forms of urban development. By 1950 this figure was 10 per cent and by 1970, 12 per cent. By 2000 it is likely to be between 15 and 16 per cent.

This prospective increase in the urban area is based on the Registrar General's expectations of population growth current in the late 1960s, and on an allowance for some lowering of average residential densities, particularly in the private sector. Lower densities are to be expected since most of the homes we are building now may well prove deficient in storage space for all the varied impedimenta that the

Regional conversions of agricultural land to urban use

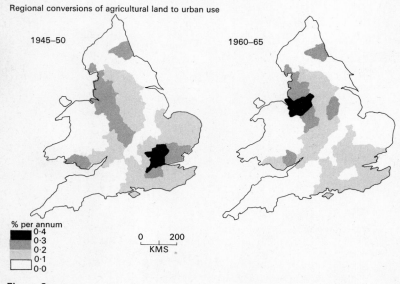

1945–50

1960–65

% per annum
0·4
0·3
0·2
0·1
0·0

0   200
KMS

Figure 2

15 and 16. *Only 12 per cent of England and Wales, according to geographer Robin Best, is currently developed for urban land uses; by the end of the century this may have risen to 16 per cent. Yet in the interests of good planning, architects since 1945 have been exhorted to squeeze more houses on to each hectare of land. They have responded with tight, cramped layouts like that at Cumbernauld new town near Glasgow. Will these homes accommodate the affluent families of the year A.D. 2000 – with perhaps two cars, a boat, camping equipment, elaborate children's toys and much other bulky impedimenta? Or shall we prove to have built millions of new slums?*

family of the year 2000 will possess; deficient too in indoor play and hobby space, not to mention garden space and car space. Houses being built today may, all too readily, degenerate into slums. But even if space standards were to rise rapidly, it seems inconceivable that we would urbanize more than about 17 or 18 per cent of our land surface. More than four in every five hectares would still be green.

Of course, the urban growth will be uneven. Most will occur where there is most urban development already – round the great conurbations and the major free-standing cities. However, Best finds no evidence that a real 'Megalopolis' is developing in England, and the most recent work from America, by Marion Clawson, indicates that Megalopolis USA is not yet a reality either. Undoubtedly, the real urban problem is occurring, and will occur, around London and Birmingham and Manchester and Bristol. It is here that there is the most difficult job of reconciling the claims of young couples for homes, of farmers for their land, and of everyone for recreation.

Considering this picture, some geographers-turned-planners may tend to take the gloomy view. They are perhaps failing to take sufficient account of some important trends – in which, with a decent time interval, Britain seems to be following the United States.

The first fact is that increasingly the location of jobs will be determined by social controls. By this I mean not the weary process of steering factory industry into the Development Areas, which Britain has tried to do with limited success since 1945, but the process of locating new public investment in things like universities and research laboratories. It is this process which has caused the mushroom growth of the American west since 1945. Paradoxically, despite the Development Area policies, in Britain the same process has built up the research and education belt which stretches west of London to embrace Reading, Harwell, and Oxford. In future, our national planners will perhaps at last grasp the self-evident truth: that in terms of potential employment growth, a new university is of far greater regional significance than a new aluminium smelter.

The second point is that for a wide range of locational decisions, the critical point is now the quality of the environment. The University Grants Committee siting a new university, an industrialist relocating his factory, the retired couple settling on their retirement home or the family contemplating a country cottage – all will be asking, first of all, whether they find the area physically and culturally pleasant. This in turn is associated with a social trend; the greater importance of leisure, and the greater value placed on using it well. This, by the way, does not necessarily reflect greater amounts of leisure; the myth of the shorter working week is rapidly being dispelled as more people work overtime or take second jobs. It does mean that as people become more affluent, they value their leisure more, and are willing to pay more to get the right environment in which to spend it.

In this search for environment, some may find the answer in the

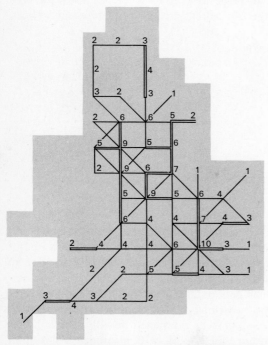

Figure 3   Lionel March's diagram of road plans for 1980. Figures show the number of connections by motorway: the higher the figure, the more accessible' the location.

congested, bustling, face-to-face world of the city. But there is plenty of evidence that most people will find their goal elsewhere. Universities, retired couples, new model factories and second home seekers: all tend to locate in the countryside, on the coast, in areas of high natural quality. This trend is fortified, in turn, by the changing technology of transportation and communication. People in increasing numbers are finding that the new motorways are offering them an astonishing freedom in the choice of where to live. A resident of the Potteries can already commute by car either to Manchester or Birmingham; when the M4 is open at the end of 1971, a resident of Newbury might work either in London or in Bristol. This process will take time to work out: it will take at least another ten years for people's perception of distance to alter on a really mass scale, and another ten years for the fact to reflect itself in estate agents' prices.

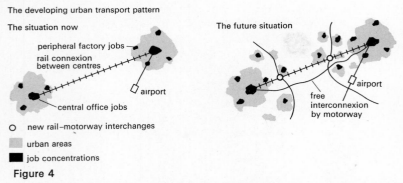

The developing urban transport pattern

The situation now

peripheral factory jobs
rail connexion between centres
airport
central office jobs

The future situation

airport
free interconnexion by motorway

O new rail-motorway interchanges

urban areas

job concentrations

Figure 4

Already, though, there are portents. The 1966 Census shows that Britain is following the pattern set by America: both people and jobs are decentralizing from the cities into the suburban rings around them on a massive scale. Land values have been rising all along the new motorways in the exurban commuter fringes round the conurbations, as along the M3 and M4 west of London, even before construction started. The M6, even though it did not penetrate fully into Cumberland and Westmorland until the end of 1970, has unleashed a flood of weekend visitors from Lancashire and even from Birmingham into the Lake District.

But transportation in a physical sense is only one way of communicating. The most dramatic change in the next twenty years will be the development of telecommunications. Already, the Post Office have exhibited a life-size mock up of the civil engineer of the 1990s at work. He sits in a luxurious office in his own country home. He communicates instantly with other professionals, with construction workers at a number of sites up and down the country, and with computer facilities, using a bewildering variety of devices: the videophone, the data transmission link, the computer visual display with light pen, the cordless telephone. He does his job with twice the efficiency he could have obtained in the old-fashioned office. And he eliminates commuting. The home has become the workplace. It could be in the Surrey Hills, it could be on the island of Mull. This, with a vengeance, could represent what Henry Ford foretold when he said: We shall deal with the problems of the city by abolishing the city.

By and large, planners are not yet fully alive to these challenges – even though so many of them were trained as geographers. Mere conservation and preservation policies are no longer enough; it is necessary to accept the new trends and plan to accommodate them. A car based society means more shopping centres of the out of town type, now pioneered in this country by the Woolco stores at Oadby (Leicester), Bournemouth and Thornaby-on-Tees. This may be unpalatable to planners who have been brought up to believe in the unique virtue of the traditional European city; yet the alternative is urban surgery which will destroy the very urban quality that the planner wants to preserve. Again, long distance car commuting means a conscious plan for village growth, and even for new commuter villages on the lines of Span's New Ash Green in Kent. It is an idea repugnant to the planner brought up in the tradition of Welwyn Garden City; but the alternative will surely be piecemeal erosion of fine villages.

The search for outdoor recreation means not merely a policy for protecting large parts of the national parks from the incursions of the motorcar – a policy being developed now by the more enlightened national parks authorities. It means also that new park facilities will need to be developed on a grand scale, ranging from the country park close to the conurbation – the new Wirral Way, created along seventeen kilometres of disused railway, is a first example – to the new national park which serves as an objective of long trips, like the projected Cotswold Water Park created out of disused gravel pits in the Thames headwaters in Gloucestershire and Wiltshire.

The new stress on amenity also means a changed policy towards agriculture. Whether or not we join the Common Market, British agriculture seems sure to continue as one of the more prosperous and efficient in Europe. But these very qualities make it an unreliable guardian of the environment. In the days not long ago, before pesticides or prairie farming, farmers were natural guardians of the ecosystem; their own self-interest demanded, and respected, certain principles of natural balance, which incidentally created one of the most memorable and most human man-made landscapes in the world. That happy equation has now gone. Not only in the eastern arable lowlands of England, but now widely across the country, farmers are happily tearing up the hedgerows their ancestors planted at the time of the enclosures, between two and five centuries ago; they are content to spray their crops with pesticides that may actually be lethal to man until they are banned by a higher authority. Their relentless drive to higher efficiency may benefit the balance of payments; the community has the right and the responsibility to decide, just as with car exhausts or factory pollution, that the price may not be worth paying. In other words, we may find ourselves paying farmers not to take up their hedgerows – just as Americans pay farmers not to grow crops, though perhaps with a more admirable reason.

Above all, we have to recognize that in an amenity conscious age, competing claims for land have to be judged in a different way. To the 19th-century economist, there was a Highest and Best Use for any parcel of land, which was found by trial and error in the free land market; even Macaulay looked forward to the day when the highlands of Britain would all be cultivated up to their summits, and only a minority doubted that muck was a price worth paying for money. Thirty years ago, in the intense burst of activity that created our planning system in Britain, some pioneers realized that these rules would no longer hold for the future; they tried to create a new set. Today, most disinterested witnesses would conclude that the

17. *Post Office mock-up of the civil engineer of the 1990s. New telecommunications make it possible for him to work from a country retreat without any need to commute to an office. These techniques – which are being tested and developed now – could mean the end of the traditional city as a centre for work.*

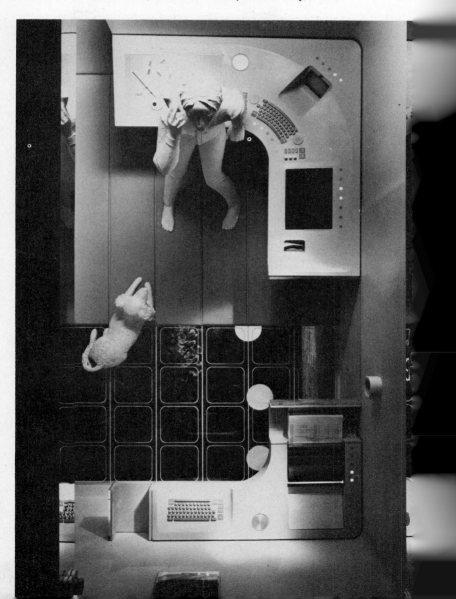

resulting system corrected some abuses, but created many of its own. In particular, it proved much stronger on the negative than on the positive side. It could stop ribbon building into the countryside; it could not guarantee that the countryside would retain its qualities, still less that it would be opened up to the recreational needs of the town dweller. It could regulate building, and thus the form of development; it could not guarantee a high standard of design. And where it was administered by vested interests, it could stifle necessary change, forcing new activities into a strait-jacket of old urban forms.

To rectify this we need a new planning system working through new authorities. The 1968 Planning Act potentially gives us the first, specifying an end to the old rigid master land use plans and providing for their replacement by new strategic plans covering broad areas; the report of the Redcliffe-Maud Commission provided the basis for the second. It is possible to have endless debate about whether the Redcliffe-Maud solution of 1969, or the two-tier solution in the 1971 White Paper, was better. The point is that any solution that can be implemented, and which abolishes the absurd division in planning between town and country, is the right solution.

What principles should guide the new authorities in preparing their new plans? Above all others, in an age of general affluence, must be the principle of access to opportunity. The characteristic feature of modern middle-class society, which is spreading to a wide stratum of prosperous blue-collar workers, here and in America, is this demand for a wide range of opportunities in every area: jobs, education, consumer services, recreation, entertainment. The key to this accessibility is, of course, mobility. Both these words – accessibility and mobility – have several possible meanings, or dimensions: we can talk of economic mobility, or social mobility, or geographic mobility. It is the geographic aspect that must particularly concern the land use planner; and it is the key to most of the other sorts. When black children in American cities are taken by bus to white schools, the bus represents the physical mobility which gives geographic accessibility to educational opportunities, and thus social and economic mobility. When a new shopping centre attracts motorized shoppers from fifty kilometres away, that again represents geographical mobility that permits greater accessibility to services, and thus permits possible changes in social life styles. By providing adequate public transport along an improved road system from a declining coal mining area to a new town thirty kilometres away, the geographical mobility confers the means to economic mobility – a change in job, and perhaps eventually a change in social life style, too.

The job of the land use planner, then, is to multiply access to all sorts of opportunity within his planning region. He has to recognize that to some extent the range of possible opportunities has to vary according to the region he is planning. The German sociologist, Erwin Scheuch, once asked people what sort of environment they would like to live in: a substantial number wanted a detached house by a lake, in its own extensive grounds, five minutes from an office job in a city centre. The job of the planner is to recognize the impracticality of that solution, and then to do his best to get as near to it as possible. He will not be able to combine maximum accessibility to executive jobs, gourmet restaurants and night clubs, with maximum accessibility to open moorland walks and salmon fishing; he will hope that those opting for the first will migrate towards the south-east, and those opting for the second will migrate towards the north or Scotland. But given that, he will aim to produce a region with the maximum accessibility to those resources that exist. In the south-east, this probably means recognizing that increasing numbers of people will combine high-density flat living in inner London during the week with low-density country living in the Weald or Berkshire Downs during the weekend, with all the consequences for land use that this implies. In the north, it means developing the night life of Newcastle while stressing the accessibility of the good river fishing, in which the region is superbly endowed.

These examples stress middle-class aspirations and middle-class choices; that is right, because that is the way, like it or not, we are going. But in the process, it is worth stressing that we will be faced with an increasing problem of relative deprivation. This is the term developed by American sociologists to describe the plight of the negro in affluent California where, when 90 per cent of the population are very rich, the other 10 per cent seem very poor – even if they are rich by the standards of the rest of the world. In an environment

where many families have two cars or even three, the possession of a
1959 Chevrolet may seem like the lowest depths of poverty. The
relevance for us is that as the standards and aspirations of the
affluent majority rise, there is the obvious danger that the bottom
10 or 20 per cent sink relatively further down.

Relative deprivation, like the opportunity and mobility which are
its counterpart, has an obvious geographical expression. At the
regional level, it is the problem of all those peripheral areas with
economic problems and social problems underlying them. Here, considerable resources will need to be pumped in just to keep them
competitive with the more affluent south. Though the state can provide resources for regional opera or good secondary education, it
will find it more difficult to subsidize regional cuisine or delicatessen
shops – which, in a materialist culture, may be even more important
in attracting people to these areas. It will take a long time for the
growth of middle-class demand in Workington or Hartlepool to
reach the standards of Hampstead or Kensington today and, by that
time, Hampstead and Kensington will be farther ahead again.

Another sort of deprivation will be more local; it too is already
evident. It is the decreasing percentage of drop-outs who remain,

18. *Artist's impression of the ideal environment as revealed by social survey:
house in own grounds, surrounded by forest, near a lake, only five minutes from
the city centre. It sounds impracticable, but it is the planner's job to do his best
to get as near to it as possible.*

mainly in the schools of certain big city neighbourhoods, when 90 per cent of the students have passed their GCE or CSE examinations. This is not fanciful; in certain parts of London, it is happening now. These drop-outs will be the most difficult of all minority groups: a group identified and branded as inferior by the standards of a meritocratic society. They will have the material demands of their better educated fellows, but none of the abilities necessary to satisfy them. Indeed, if American experience provides a parallel, they may be virtually unemployable in a computerized, professionalized society. They may provide a fertile breeding ground for crime and social malaise of all kinds. They represent the lack of any kind of mobility – or of access to opportunity – in its starkest form.

One hundred years ago, Britain's future still seemed to be based on coal and iron. But already, the challenge of other countries was forcing us into the first tentative experiment in universal education. Today, material resources seem strangely irrelevant to Britain's future. Even the richest North Sea gas strike is of little consequence compared with the education that brings advanced skills, or the resources of environment. In a world where education and tourism are probably the fastest growing industries, Britain is favourably placed in terms of resources. But the lesson for the future is that these resources can, and must, be exploited through deliberate policies.

References

Best, R., 'The Future Urban Acreage', *Town and Country Planning*, 32, 1964 pp. 350–5.

Best, R., and Champion, A. G., 'Regional Conversions of Agricultural Land to Urban Use in England and Wales, 1945–67', *Transactions of the Institute of British Geographers*, 49, 1970, pp. 15–32.

Clawson, M., *Suburban Land Conversion in the United States*, Johns Hopkins, 1971.

Cowan, P., (ed.), *Developing Patterns of Urbanization*, Oliver and Boyd, 1970.

Hall, P., Drewett, R., Gracey, H., and Thomas, R., *Megalopolis Denied*, Allen & Unwin, 1971.

Hall, P., 'The Urban Culture and the Suburban Culture', in Richard Eells and Clarence Walton (eds.), *Man in the City of the Future*, Macmillan, 1969, pp. 99–145.

March, L., *The Spatial Organisation of Hyper-Urban Society*, Town and Country Planning Summer School, 1969.

Stone, P. A., *Urban Growth in Britain: standards, costs and resources, 1964–2004*. Vol. I, *Population Trends and Housing*, CUP, 1970.

Acknowledgements

The publishers wish to thank the following for permission to use their photographs: Peter Keen for plates 1 and 2; John Topham Ltd for plates 3 and 4; the Mersey Docks and Harbour Board for plate 5; Terence Wilson and Partners for plate 6; the Ford Motor Company for plate 7; the Central Electricity Generating Board for plates 8 and 9; the British Steel Corporation for plate 10; D. R. Parker for plate 11; the United Kingdom Atomic Energy Authority for plate 12; Fairey Surveys Ltd for plate 13; Picturepoint Ltd (to whom copyright is reserved) for plate 14; the British Aluminium Company for plate 15; the Basildon Development Corporation for plate 16; the Council for Industrial Design for plate 17; the *Geographical Magazine* for plate 18.

The drawings in the chapter entitled *LEISURE AND THE COUNTRYSIDE: the Example of the Dartmoor National Park* were produced by the drawing offices of the Joint School of Geography, King's College, London, and the London School of Economics.

More about Penguins and Pelicans

Penguinews, which appears every month, contains details of all the new books issued by Penguins as they are published. From time to time it is supplemented by *Penguins in Print*, which is a complete list of all books published by Penguins which are in print. (There are well over three thousand of these.)

A specimen copy of *Penguinews* will be sent to you free on request, and you can become a subscriber for the price of the postage. For a year's issues (including the complete lists) please send 30p if you live in the United Kingdom, or 60p if you live elsewhere. Just write to Dept EP, Penguin Books Ltd, Harmondsworth, Middlesex, enclosing a cheque or postal order, and your name will be added to the mailing list.

Some other books published by Penguins are described on the following pages.

Note: *Penguinews* and *Penguins in Print* are not available in the U.S.A. or Canada

Britain in Figures

A HANDBOOK OF SOCIAL STATISTICS

Alan F. Sillitoe

This handbook of statistical graphs and diagrams, with explanatory texts, has been prepared by a sociologist to illustrate recent and current social trends in Britain (with foreign figures for comparison). It makes the perfect tool for quick reference on the desk and for settling arguments in the home.

Population – Growth, ages, expectation of life, deaths, density, immigration

Social Data – Marriage, divorce, pensions, house-building, religion

Education – Numbers at schools and universities, examination passes, expenditure

Labour – Hours worked, Trade Unions, strikes, unemployment

The Economy – Public and private expenditure, prices, incomes, taxation, inflation, exports and imports

Transport & Communications – Cars, telephones etc., road deaths, road-building

Mass Media – Newspapers, radio, television, cinemas and their audiences

Guide to the British Economy

Peter Donaldson

Guide to the British Economy is intended for the general reader who would like to have some grasp of what economics is about and what makes the economy tick, but who may find the textbook approach unpalatably abstract. Economic ideas, therefore, are presented here within the real context of the British economy. The aim is both to give an impression of the working of the different elements in the economy, and to illustrate the extent to which economic analysis can be helpful in solving the problems which face policy-makers.

In the first part of this introductory guide Peter Donaldson is mainly concerned with matters of finance, including the stock-market. After a full examination of industry, labour, and trade, he goes on, in the final section of the book, to a general discussion of economic theories, their scope and limitations.

Geology and Scenery in England and Wales

A. E. Trueman

Why the country looks as it does interests the motorist and the holiday-maker as much as geological structure concerns the student. This Pelican explains very simply why some districts are wooded and others cultivated; why rivers often take the long way round to the sea; why hills may be jagged or rounded; why features like Wenlock Edge or the Chilterns run from north-east to south-west, and a thousand other cases where the landscape of England and Wales is decided by the underlying strata.

Geology and its allied sciences have not stood still since Sir Arthur Trueman's study established itself as a little classic many years ago. For this new edition the whole book has been thoroughly revised, to take account of recent findings, by Drs Whittow and Hardy of Reading University. They have completely rewritten several sections and replaced the drawings with appropriate photographs.

Much however, of Sir Arthur's delightful text still stands in a book which makes an anti-clockwise tour of the country from the Cotswold Stone Belt and the Chalklands to the granite cliffs and moors of Cornwall and Devon, describing each region in fascinating detail.

The Geography of World Affairs

J. P. Cole

This book, which has now been completely revised and brought up-to-date, sets out to help the reader who is not a specialist in geography to find his way about the world and to provide him with facts about the location, population, size, and activities of the more important countries in it. Most of the material in this book is geographical in nature, but many questions cannot be considered, even from a purely geographical viewpoint, without reference to history, politics, and economics.